Design Games for Architecture

Design Games for Architecture teaches you how to create playful software tools based on your architectural design processes, whether or not you are familiar with game design technology. The book combines the fun and engaging aspects of video games to ease the sometimes complex process of learning software development. By working through six exercises illustrated with screen shots and code, you acquire knowledge about each step required to build useful tools you can use to accomplish design tasks. Steps include analyzing design processes to identify their logic, translating that logic into a collection of objects and functions, then encoding the design procedure into a working software tool. Examples presented in the book are design games – tools that a designer "plays" like video games – that span a wide range of design activities. These software tools are built using Unity: free, innovative and industry-leading software for video game development. Unity speeds up the process of software creation, offers an interface that will be familiar to you, and includes very advanced tools for creating forms, effects and interactivity. If you are looking to add cutting-edge skills to your repertoire, then *Design Games* will help you sharpen your design thinking and allow you to specialize in this new territory while you learn more about your own design processes.

Aaron Westre is an adjunct instructor at the University of Minnesota School of Architecture and founder of Artificial Natures, a design studio specializing in building custom software for architects and designers.

Design Games for Architecture

Creating Digital Design Tools with Unity

Aaron Westre

 Routledge
Taylor & Francis Group

NEW YORK AND LONDON

1006957837

First published 2014
by Routledge
711 Third Avenue, New York, NY 10017

Simultaneously published in the UK
by Routledge
2 Park Square, Milton Park, Abingdon, Oxon OX14 4RN

Routledge is an imprint of the Taylor & Francis Group, an informa business

Library of Congress Cataloging in Publication Data
Westre, Aaron.
Design games for architecture : creating digital design tools with Unity / Aaron Westre.
pages cm
Includes index.
1. Architecture--Study and teaching. 2. Architecture--Problems, exercises, etc. 3. Computer games--Programming. 4. Unity (Electronic resources) I. Title.
NA2005.W47 2013
720.285--dc23
2013003836

ISBN: 978-0-415-62276-9 (hbk)
ISBN: 978-0-415-62277-6 (pbk)
ISBN: 978-0-203-75017-9 (ebk)

Acquisition Editor: Wendy Fuller
Editorial Assistant: Laura Williamson
Production Editor: Alanna Donaldson

Typeset in Bembo by
Servis Filmsetting Ltd, Stockport, Cheshire

Printed in Great Britain by Bell & Bain Ltd, Glasgow

Dedication

Many people were instrumental throughout the writing of this book. Thank you to Polly, whose unending support was critical to my progress. Thank you to J, whose experience and pragmatism helped refine my approach. Thank you to the University of Minnesota School of Architecture for giving me the opportunity to experiment with and refine these ideas.

Contents

Contents

Figures

Introduction

The idea for this book emerged out of a course I teach at the University of Minnesota School of Architecture. Design Games is the title of the course and my goal in creating it was to teach architecture students how to develop software. On the face of it, this seems like a rather odd thing to do in a school of architecture. My students had no prior experience building software and were not even particularly interested in learning the skill. Yet registration for the course was enthusiastic. Why? The reason has to do with some not-so-subtle subterfuge on my part. I structured the course entirely around video gaming. The very first assignment required students to play a video game and report back to the class their experience. This is a great way to start a semester. Maybe a bit too great considering the rest of the course involves building software, a difficult task for anyone to learn, let alone designers. Yet the students who take the course invariably achieve amazing results in just a few weeks. They leave the course empowered by a new skill and a new way of thinking about the process of design. This is due to the type of software they make.

Teams of students are tasked with constructing a type of software I've coined a design game. A design game is a hybrid: part video game, part design tool. Being a design tool, its primary purpose is to assist a designer in a particular task by increasing their productivity or opening up new creative possibilities. Not simply tools, design games incorporate elements from video games to engage designers in more creative, social and playful ways. I ask my students to use three words as primary criteria when making their design games: simple, engaging and instrumental. A design game is simple because it should assist a designer in a single task in the design process. This keeps the scope of the project manageable and focuses attention on functionality. A design game is engaging due to the techniques it incorporates from the world of video games. It might be more visually striking to draw in the designer, it might foster creativity by playfully interacting with the designer or it might introduce productive constraints such as points, timers or lives into the design process. A design game is instrumental because it produces some concrete design outcome. This could be a three-dimensional (3D) form that serves as the inspiration for a design, a finished component of a design to be fabricated or anything that helps a designer move to the next step in their process. These three criteria could be summed up by saying that a design game is a playful tool.

After teaching this course several times, I have witnessed a wide variety of design games come into being. There are practical examples like a game that combines the action of Tetris® with the task of floor planning. Others tend more toward the absurd such as one called Zombietecture in which players create forms by killing – you guessed it – zombies. Some encourage casual engagement such as a sculpting game requiring players to 'fish' for shapes by 'casting' with a Wii® remote. Analysis is another trend, as in a design game that allows architects to crowdsource the evaluation of the accessibility of their designs. Some have very tangible outcomes, like a tool that allows designers to fabricate lathed forms that result from a simple game. Results from other design games are more abstract, as in History's Mysteries, which teaches the history of famous architectural landmarks. Regardless of the purpose, focus or seriousness of these and the many other design games created in the course, there are common threads that connect them all. Each one represents the students' careful analysis of a specific design task and their encoding of that task into a tool. They all present an alternative model of design software, one that focuses more on purpose-built and personal tools. Ultimately they all represent an approach to toolmaking that values playfulness as a source of creativity, insight and productivity.

The idea of design games is not a new one. A good example would be SimCity®, a game essentially about city planning. Players make decisions about budgets, distribution of housing and placement of services. Eventually they evolve their virtual cities either toward peaceful prosperity or collapse. If SimCity® had an export function by which the player could assemble and distribute their ideal city plan, it would fit the definition of a design game perfectly.

Why Combine Video Games with Design Tools?

A design game, despite its name, doesn't need to be a game per se. Points, levels, time limits and the like can be incorporated, but a player doesn't really need to 'win' a design game. This is because design games are ultimately tools, and as such they need to be open-ended enough to allow a designer to arrive at a wide variety of outcomes. If the rules of the game are too restrictive, the outcomes will in turn be deterministic and repetitive. If a tool can only produce a few outcomes its utility to a designer will be limited. They may use it a few times, but it's unlikely that it will become a valued tool in their design process. If the requirements for making a game are relaxed, more exploratory tools can be produced that retain many of the aspects that make games fun. The ideal design game forgoes the strict win–or–lose narrative of video games while instilling the design process with the same playfulness that video games so readily promote.

The techniques used in the design of video games represent an enormous, untapped resource that could be used in creating new types of design tools. The video game industry has developed these techniques over the course of several decades and employs them to great success today. Some of the technology developed for the video game industry (as well as film) has made its way into the design world. Examples include animation software like Maya® and Blender. Likewise most designers have benefited from increases in computer graphics power, largely driven by video gaming, to improve their representations with rendering applications. Yet many of the innovations of the video game industry have so far gone unexploited in the realm of digital design tools.

One of the things video games do really well is lowering their players' aversion to failing. When my car crashes in a racing game or my avatar is shot in a first person shooter, I'm presented with the spectacular, if sometimes gory, scene of my own failure. Instead of acting as a deterrence, these spectacular failures actually spur players on to continue their quest. This seeming paradox is due to a couple of key aspects. First, failure in video games rarely spells the end of play. Multiple lives and other types of second chances mean that failure in a video game doesn't carry with it the same repercussions as it does in real life. With the cost of failure lowered, players are much more likely to carry out risky, but potentially rewarding, actions. Second, when a player fails in a video game, the very reason for that failure is embedded in what they see on the screen. A player may miss their mark when trying to jump over a chasm, but as they plummet to their doom they will almost always notice some crucial miscalculation. They might figure out they didn't run fast enough or jump at the correct time or they notice a bridge that they didn't see before. In this moment the player learns a valuable piece of information. Upon receiving another chance at the task, this learning offers the player a powerful enticement to try again with new knowledge in hand. This simple feedback mechanism rewards exploration and iteration, two attitudes that are also valuable in the design process. In contrast, the design software on the market today lacks any such feedback mechanism. Of course tools like 3D modelers and other computer-aided design (CAD) systems were never intended to behave like this. They are instead intended to be generic and powerful tools for representing designs. It is an intriguing exercise, however, to imagine design tools that employed this kind of feedback to encourage more intense and playful experimentation.

Another unique quality that video games possess, as opposed to other types of software, is incredible ease-of-use. Without the aid of manuals, tutorials or instructional videos, players develop expertise in new games quite rapidly. To illustrate this, compare the time it took for you to become competent with the last CAD application you learned to the last video game you played. Barring the few exceptions that are sure to arise, the time invested in learning a CAD application generally far exceeds that of video games. The reasons for this disparity start with the environments they present to their users. When a player first starts a new video game they are presented with a very rich and engaging environment. Cues as to what to do are embedded in a seamless fashion into that environment: tips on how to move, highlighted targets and quick explanations of the mission. All of these cues combine to leave the player with a very strong sense of their role in the game and how to begin filling it. The rapid gains in understanding are compounded in most games by making the first few tasks a player completes simple and easily accomplished. These first few simple tasks are known as quick wins – easily conquered missions that show a player the ropes and entice them to continue. Quick wins offer very important feedback that help a player gain proficiency at an accelerated rate and move on to the next level. Embedded cues in the environment and quick wins could be useful in many areas of design software. Think of the time that could be saved by turning CAD software tutorials into games. If, on first opening the software, a designer was presented with a very clear set of tasks and rich feedback on their progress, the learning process could be greatly accelerated.

Potentially useful techniques can be gleaned from video games of all scales. While large scale, 3D, mission-based games offer a variety of innovations, a type particularly interesting in the context of this book is casual games. Intended to be played for short bursts of time, casual games occupy the opposite extreme from the epic first-person-shooters and strategy games. Popular examples include web and mobile phone games like the Bejeweled® series or Angry Birds®. They are typically centered on puzzle solving activities, but the content is of less importance here than some of their other aspects. Most popular design software is intended to encompass a large percentage of the activities in which a designer engages. Think about the image editors, 3D modelers or other software that plays a starring role in a designer's workday. Casual games offer a model for a different kind of design tool. They are visually engaging, very fun and yet they are not serious. A player can pick up the game, play for 5 minutes and put it back down again without having to worry about losing points or missions. The game is always ready for them at the point where they left off. A class of design tools based on this model might include a wide array of useful, game-like utilities that could exist alongside the more primary software. Casual design games could offer brief diversions, bursts of inspiration, useful insights or other helpful tidbits throughout a designer's day. Tournament style games that help a designer quickly choose a color combination or a geometric pattern, physics games that test structural ideas, or simple and playful sculpting tools are just a few of the many options.

While the argument so far has focused on the potential benefit of design games to the individual designer, it leaves out the social aspect of games. It is becoming more and more difficult to find a video game made today that does not in some way incorporate this social aspect. Whether massively multiplayer online role-playing games like World of Warcraft® or more casual web-based games like FarmVille® on Facebook®, nearly all games now are social. Social games introduce collective goals, accountability to the group, conversation, negotiation, shared memories and many other aspects of collective action. Adding this social aspect to games makes for richer and more engaging play, as evidenced by the popularity of multi-player games. They are so successful that it seems the term multi-player may soon be obsolete as more and more games take advantage of the social dynamic to enrich players' experiences. Design tools, on the other hand, lie mostly in the single-player domain (if you don't count your co-worker looking over your shoulder). What would the world of social design tools look and feel like? Perhaps it's a virtual room where collaborators can critique and modify a shared 3D model. Maybe it's more like a designer's version of Rock Band® in which each collaborator wields a different instrument that creates forms and patterns. Collective action is such a powerful force in the gaming world that it seems past its time in design, a discipline that is so fundamentally social.

Another reason for investigating this idea of design games lies in the act of developing the software itself. The prospect of learning programming and other software development knowledge is quite daunting, especially to students with no technical background or inclination. Developing software that has the qualities of a game makes this complex process more approachable and engaging. While still a formidable goal, creating a game doesn't seem quite as intimidating as creating software with a more serious overtone. Games are also something that everyone understands. When a student creates a design game, their work is immediately comprehensible to a wide variety of people. A great deal of pride can be derived from accomplishing a task as hard as creating a software application, but when it can be easily shared with others that pride grows tremendously. A deeper reason resides in the similarity between the design process and games. Just as rules, constraints, exploration and playfulness define games, the same could be said of the process of design. When this similarity is realized, it becomes a simple matter of translation to turn a design process into something resembling a video game.

I wonder as well about the new types of designers that could emerge through this linkage of design and gaming. If enough design games were available in enough places, there could be whole new segments of people that might become interested in pursuing careers in design. A student exposed to traditional design practices and not finding much of interest may well play a design game or two and change their mind. There is also the possibility that design games could reach places where design education is not available at all, making them the only exposure a student might have. Others still might be attracted by the technical aspects that arise when design is combined with computers. There could be a diverse new population of designers with new interests and motivations inspired by this intersection of games and design.

Why Should Designers Learn to Develop Software?

First it's necessary to examine what makes up a tool. At its most basic, a tool is simply a device used to accomplish a specific task. The archetypical example of the hammer works well here: a tough head joined to a shaft that allows a person to apply a great deal of pressure to a small area by swinging their arm. Given this description, a tool could also be described as a device that extends human capacities. A person swinging their fist can exert only a certain amount of force on a point, but with a hammer they greatly increase that capacity. Another way to conceptualize a tool is to think of the process that it represents. The hammer in this case arises by someone translating the desire to exert a large amount of pressure on a small area by creating an object by which a person can carry out this task. A tool is a process embodied in an object. The object in a sense encodes the process for which it is meant.

Software, though much more complex than a hammer, is no different. By encoding a process in a specific syntax (programming), software can be created to carry out nearly any arbitrary task. The computer acts as a generic platform on which any type of tool can be created. Design software today typically encodes hundreds of processes. Each of these is a tool unto itself, encoding processes such as draw a line, create a volume, cut, copy or paste. These are generic functions. The reason why 3D modeling and graphics software is so popular is that in these applications hundreds of the most common, and therefore most useful, operations are encoded. It's the reason why most designers use a common set of software tools. There are, however, still many tasks that those tools do not, and cannot, accommodate. These are the tasks that call out for a custom tool, one that will make the design process simpler, more comprehensible and more attuned to the designer's intention. By learning a bit about software development, designers can understand what's possible and when creating a custom tool might be very beneficial.

Creating custom software can be a very empowering experience. There is a substantial learning curve, but the benefits outweigh the costs. New tools exist that make building software into a process much more familiar to designers. Unity, the development environment used in this book, is one such tool. Whereas software development in the past was accomplished primarily through programming, new software like Unity makes programming just one part of a larger process. These new software development tools present the potential developer with much more visually oriented interfaces that put placing 3D models, editing images and setting parameters on the same plane as programming. Creating software becomes much more like the processes that designers are already familiar with, lowering the barrier to enter this previously confusing and technical territory.

Ultimately, the best reason for a designer to educate themselves about software development is what that learning teaches them about their own design process. Making software that encodes a specific design process requires a rigorous analysis of that process. Because software works on the logic embedded in it, the intentions of its designer must be clear or the software won't work. The rigor required mandates a concrete knowledge of the process in question. By examining their design process to this degree, a designer can arrive at a new understanding of that process. Extraneous tasks might be found. A step might have been overlooked. When the software starts to work as expected, the designer has validated their thinking about the process. Even if the exercise in software development goes no further, some important insights into the designer's own process were gleaned.

Who Is This Book For?

This book is written for students, faculty and practitioners of design interested in exploring making their own software tools. I come from the discipline of architecture, so the examples in this book deal with 3D design tasks. They are not so specific to architecture to not be useful to a wide variety of designers, particularly those dealing with 3D design challenges. Students of design wishing to expand their skill set into new territory should find this book useful. Learning software development can sharpen design thinking and open up new possibilities for specialization. Faculty in design fields looking to expand their exploration into computational design can also acquire useful knowledge. The book can be adapted as a curriculum for a course exploring the concept of design games or a short workshop on encoding design processes into software. Practicing designers wanting to explore software development can use this book as a reference or simply a collection of ideas from which to draw.

How Is This Book Organized?

The next chapter introduces the tools and techniques used throughout the book. It's an important chapter to read in order to understand the primary concepts that will be built on later. The bulk of the book consists of example design games and instruction on how to build them. Building Blocks and Slingshot present examples that can be used during the initial, conceptual stage of design. Kirigami and Component Lab explore examples that deal with structure and physics. Showroom demonstrates techniques for communicating architectural designs.

1

TOOLS OF THE TRADE

In the following chapters I will present several example design games and explain how they are built. For each example I will examine the design task that the tool addresses, how to analyze that task for its constituent parts and how that analysis gets translated into working software. But before getting into those examples, which constitute the bulk of this book, I need to discuss the software that you will be using to build them.

The only software necessary to complete the exercises in this book is called Unity. Unity is a software development environment used to create video games. A software development environment is like a one-stop-shop for creating software. Instead of relying on a variety of different applications to assemble files, write code and package the final product, Unity and other software like it gather all of these functions into a single place. This eliminates much of the confusion that is involved in hunting down many tools each providing a different function. Unity gathers a wide variety of very powerful capabilities into a single package. This includes a physics engine for simulating movement and collisions, advanced lighting for achieving realistic scenes, effects like fire and water, and many other cutting-edge technologies that have emerged from the video game industry. Unity also makes it easy to distribute games to PC and Mac computers, onto websites, mobile phones and video game consoles like the Nintendo Wii. The developers who created Unity are constantly adding amazing new features and adding more devices on which Unity games can run. Some of the advanced features require Unity Pro, which professional developers can purchase to create commercial video games. Luckily there is a free version that allows new developers to learn the technology, make use of most of the capabilities of Unity and distribute the software they create to computers and websites. This free version is the one you will need to complete the exercises in this book. It runs on Windows and Mac operating systems.

Let's get started. Download and install the software by going to the Unity website:

http://www.unity3d.com/

Once Unity is installed, start it up and you should see something like the screen in Figure 1.1.

When Unity is first started an example project called Bootcamp is opened automatically. It serves as an introduction to the kinds of things that Unity is capable of producing. For those readers who have used 3D modeling software, the Unity interface should look somewhat familiar. The largest pane,

Learn the basics about how Unity works and tips about the exercise in Chapter 1 on the companion website:

www.routledge.com/cw/westre

If the project doesn't open, select Asset Store from the Window menu and search for Bootcamp.

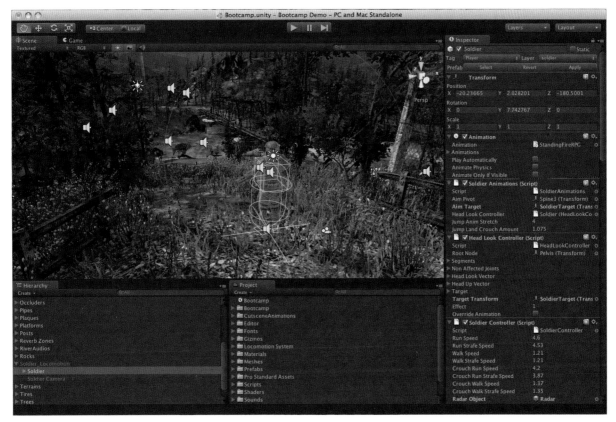

Fig. 1.1 The Unity development environment.

called the Scene View, shows the scene currently being edited and allows the developer to move around and position objects. Around the Scene View are several other views, each labeled at the top with their name. In the lower left corner, the Hierarchy lists all of the objects in the current scene. Each object in the scene can be selected either by clicking on it in the Scene View or by clicking its name in the Hierarchy. In the middle is the Project View which lists all of the assets that can be used in the project. Assets are files like 3D models, images, videos and sounds. Dragging an asset from the Project View to either the Scene View or the Hierarchy places it into the current scene. The Inspector, on the right, lists all of the data about the currently selected object in the scene. This data consists of parameters like position, rotation and scale along with any materials that alter the object's appearance or scripts that give the object behaviors. The Inspector is where all of the different aspects of an object's look and behavior can be modified. The arrangement of all of these views can be changed by selecting an option in the Layout menu, but for the purposes of this book I will be using the default layout called Wide.

Fig. 1.2 Transform Tools – From left to right: hand, translate, rotate and scale.

Fig. 1.3 Play Mode Tools – From left to right: play, pause and step.

At the top of the Unity window is the Toolbar containing buttons and menus for some commonly used functions. The elements most frequently used are the Transform Tools and the Play Mode buttons.

If you click the hand button in the Transform Tools, then click and drag anywhere in the Scene View, your view of the scene will pan up, down, left or right depending on where you drag the mouse. Hold down the Alt key on the keyboard while dragging and the view will rotate similarly to rotating your head. If you hold down the control (Ctrl) key, you can zoom in and out of the scene. Zooming can also be accomplished by scrolling with a mouse or trackpad, just as with scrolling up and down in a webpage or document. The translate, rotate and scale tools to the right of the hand tool allow the selected object to be moved around the scene, rotated and resized respectively. Try clicking on an object in the scene to select it, then using each of these tools to move, rotate and resize the object. The Play Mode Tools control previewing how the game looks and functions. The play button starts the game, the pause button halts the action and the step button advances a single frame. Click the play button to see what the Bootcamp game feels like. In the game use the arrow keys to move around, the space bar to jump and click in the scene to have the soldier fire his gun. When you are finished you can exit play mode by clicking the play button once more.

There are obviously many more features of the Unity interface that I haven't described. Many of these will come up in the following chapters and some are beyond the scope of this book. The important outcome here is to become familiar with the names of the most useful pieces of the interface, as they come up frequently throughout this book. The support section of the Unity website offers information on all aspects of the interface as well as instructions on basic techniques and in-depth tutorials on advanced topics. It is a valuable resource that comes directly from the people who made the software. I strongly encourage readers to refer to the Unity website in addition to the instruction provided in this book.

Trying It Out

Create a new project by selecting New Project from the File menu. Unity will ask if you want to save the Bootcamp project, but you can click Don't Save.

The Project Wizard window will appear. Unity will give your project a default location and name. If you want to change these, click the Set button,

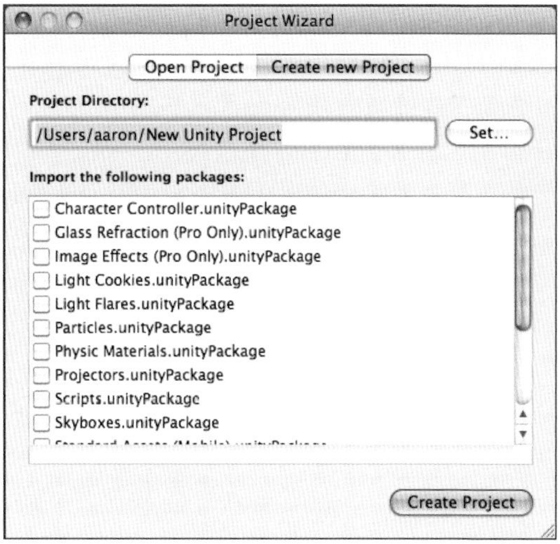

Fig. 1.4 Project Wizard window.

type in a new name like FirstProject and select the folder where you want the project saved. The folder where you store your Unity projects is up to you and Unity will show all of your past projects when you choose Open Project from the File menu. Once the name and location of the project folder are set, click the Create Project button.

Your new project will look quite a bit more stark than the Bootcamp project. New projects in Unity have only one lonely object in the scene, the camera through which the player will look during the game called Main Camera. You can see what this view looks like by pressing the play button. Pressing play once again will return you from that empty blue world back into editing mode. In the Hierarchy, click on Main Camera to select it.

Three things happen once the camera is selected: a preview of what the camera sees appears in the bottom-right corner of the Scene View, a wireframe pyramid appears in the scene and the Inspector displays the camera's properties. The pyramid that appears is called a frustum. Its purpose is to visually show what is inside the camera's field of view. The tools in the Inspector show the variety of parameters that can alter the camera's position, view and many other factors. For instance, the blue backdrop that the camera sees can be altered by clicking on the swatch of color to the right of Background in the Inspector.

In the Color window that appears, you can choose any color and see that change reflected in the Camera Preview.

Now that changes have been made to the scene, you should save it by selecting **File > Save Scene** or by typing Control-S (Command-S on

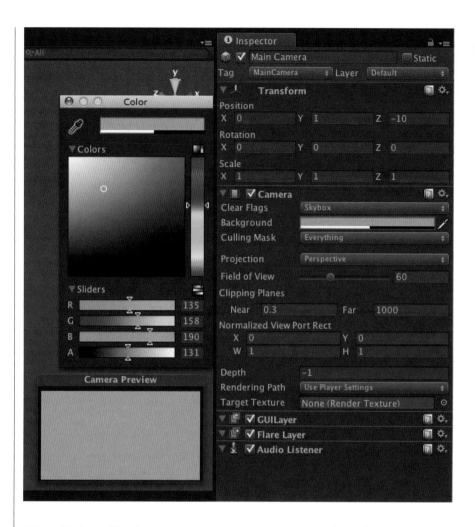

Fig. 1.5 Changing the camera's background color.

Mac). Unity will ask you to name your scene; something like MainScene will suffice. The scene will be saved in the assets folder of your project and will appear in the Project View. The reason why you have to save both the project and the scene is that Unity projects can have multiple scenes. This is useful when making games with multiple levels or environments. The examples in this book will use only one scene.

It's time to add an object to the scene. Unity has a number of built-in objects: primitive volumes like cubes and spheres, particle systems like fire and even configurable trees. In the interest of keeping things simple, add a cube by selecting **GameObject > Create Other > Cube**. A cube should appear in the scene and in the Hierarchy. In order to position the cube so that the camera has a good view of it, you have to know where the camera is and in what direction it's looking. Clicking on Main Camera in the

Hierarchy displays the camera's position as x = 0, y = 1, z = −10 (0, 1, −10) in the Inspector. By selecting the cube in the Hierarchy you can change its location by typing new values into the x, y and z boxes under Position in the Inspector.

Fig. 1.6 Setting the cube's position.

Setting the cube's position to the point (0, 1, −5) should ensure the camera a good view. Objects can also be positioned using translate in the Transform Tools and dragging the object to the desired location. Often setting positions in the Inspector is faster and more precise, but both methods are equally useful. Click the play button to see the cube centered in the camera's view.

A useful object to add at this point would be a light. There are three different types of lights available in Unity: directional lights, point lights and spot lights. Each one illuminates objects in a scene in a unique way and are useful in different circumstances. A point light is easy to work with at this stage since it casts its light equally in all directions. Add a point light to your scene by selecting **GameObject > Create Other > Point Light**. You will see a new light in the center of your scene. Making sure the point light is selected in the Hierarchy, click the translate button in the Transform Tools. Arrows appear extending from the light to indicate that it can be moved.

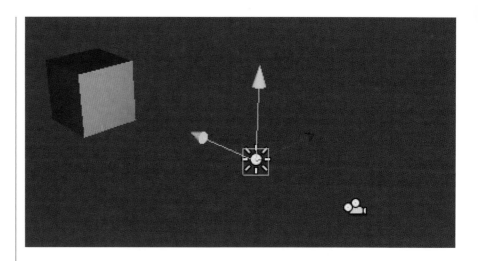

Fig. 1.7 Positioning a light using the translate gizmo.

Clicking and dragging any of these arrows will move the light along the corresponding direction. Experiment a bit with moving the light around the scene this way. Pay attention to how the cube is illuminated as the light moves. Once the cube is lit so that its faces are distinct, you've found a good spot for the light.

The cube in your scene should be able to do something besides look lonely. This is where adding behavior through scripting enters the picture. A script in Unity is a bit of code that gives an object instructions on how to behave. These behaviors can be continuous or triggered at certain times, through interaction with other objects or by receiving input from the player. There are other ways to add behavior to objects, such as physics, but that's for a later chapter. Scripting is an essential activity in making games lively, interactive and fun. Scripts in Unity can be written in a variety of different programming languages, but the examples in this book will use JavaScript. The documentation on the Unity website uses JavaScript primarily, making it an obvious choice, but there are other benefits as well. Originally invented to add interactivity to websites, JavaScript has since been adapted for a number of different programming tasks. Since it is so widely used on the web, many people learn it while figuring out how to build websites. It's one of the most widely used programming languages today. Learning a bit about how JavaScript is used can be great knowledge to have in many different situations.

To create a script, select **Assets > Create > JavaScript**. A new item called newbehaviourscript will appear in the Project View. Clicking on it will show its minimal contents in the Inspector. Clicking the Edit button in

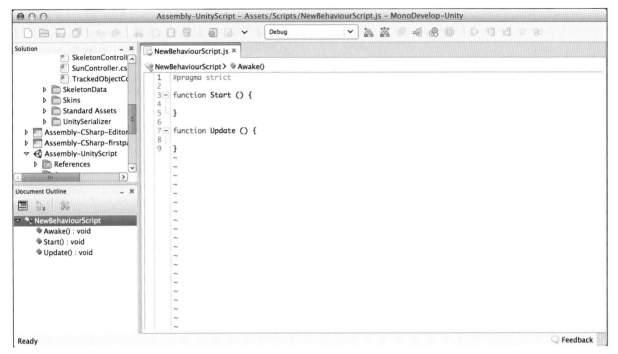

Fig. 1.8 The MonoDevelop editor displaying a newly created script.

the Inspector will launch the Unity script editor called MonoDevelop. Here you can see that the new script contains only a couple of lines.

The word function in this code is a special term in JavaScript; it signals the start of a set of instructions that can be set in motion by calling this function by name. The name of the function in this case is 'Update'. It is a function that gets called every single frame, a frame being a step in time, while a game is being played. The pair of parentheses after the name serves a purpose that will be explored more later, but in essence the parentheses act as a way to supply additional information to the rest of the function. The curly braces denote the beginning and end of the function's instructions.

The purpose of a function is as straightforward as the word function itself. It's a block of code that carries out a specific task. In Unity each object in a scene can have multiple scripts, each with multiple functions that give that object new actions that it can carry out. Thinking about a car as an object in a Unity scene is illustrative. A car would need functions that allow it to accelerate, break, shift gears and turn its headlights on. Similarly, each function in a script gives an object specific abilities. By adding a few simple instructions to the script in the editor, you can give the cube in your scene new behaviors. For example, to cause the cube to rotate only requires one additional line of code.

Listing 1.1 Rotation script.

```
function Update ()
{
    gameObject.transform.Rotate(Vector3.up * 0.5);
}
```

Add this new line to your script exactly as it is, then save the script by selecting **File > Save** or typing Control-S (Command-S on Mac). Leave the editor window open and return to the main Unity window. In order to give the cube the new behavior defined in this script, it has to be attached to the cube. To do this, drag and drop the newbehaviorscript from the Project View onto the Cube in the Hierarchy. If you've done this correctly you should see the script listed in the Inspector when the cube is selected in the Hierarchy. Click play to see the cube rotating.

Fig. 1.9 Attaching a script to an object by dragging and dropping.

The term **gameObject** at the start of the added line is a Unity variable that stands in for the current object, in this case the cube. The period that follows (referred to as a dot in programming) means there is a relationship between the two terms on either side of it. Specifically it says that the term on the right belongs to, is a part of, the term on the left. Here the term transform is a part of gameObject. The word transform is another Unity variable that refers to the position, rotation and scale data of an object. The term Rotate, which according to the dot must be part of transform, is a function that manipulates that data. In order to do its job the Rotate function needs some information called an argument that gets put in the parentheses that follow the function name. In this case the argument consists of a vector, or direction, multiplied by a number. For the Rotate function this means spin the cube around the up, or y, axis at a slow and steady pace. Finally, the semicolon at the end of the line denotes the end of a statement. Which lines need semicolons and which don't can seem arbitrary at first, but this will become clearer as things progress.

By adding a few more lines of code the cube can become more interactive. Objects in a Unity game can respond to a variety of inputs from the player. Using the listing below as a guide, modify the newbehaviorscript to include the new lines of code.

Listing 1.2 Adding interactivity.

```
function Update ()
{
    gameObject.transform.Rotate(Vector3.up * 0.5);
}

function OnMouseUp()
{
    var new_x = Random.Range(-5.0, 5.0);
    var new_y = Random.Range(-5.0, 5.0);
    var new_position = Vector3(new_x, new_y, -5.0);
    Instantiate(gameObject,
                    new_position,
                    Quaternion.identity);
}
```

As you can see, a new function OnMouseUp has been added to the script. This is a function that gets triggered whenever a player clicks on the object to which the script is attached. Inside the OnMouseUp function (within the curly braces) there are a few lines of code that serve as instructions for making a copy of the cube at a new, random location. Be sure to save the newbehaviorscript, then return to the main Unity window and click play to enter play mode. Clicking on the spinning cube will produce a copy nearby. Repeat this several times to see the screen fill up with rotating cubes. Click play again to return to editing mode.

In order to allow the cube to make copies of itself, the script needs to specify where those new copies should be located. The first two lines inside the OnMouseUp function define temporary variables called new_x and new_y. A variable is basically a word that can refer to a number, string of characters, objects in a scene or any number of other values. Because it stands in for a value, it can be used multiple times throughout a script to refer to that value instead of having to retype the value over again. Here new_x and new_y are assigned random values between −5.0 and 5.0 using the Random.Range function. These two values represent how far away from the original cube the new copy should be placed, horizontally and vertically respectively. In the next line new_x and new_y are used to create a new variable called new_position. This new variable is set equal to a type of value called a Vector3. A Vector3 contains a list of three numbers that can be used to define a point or a direction in space. Here new_x and new_y are combined with the number −5.0 to define a point that will serve as the copied cube's position.

After new_position is defined, a function named Instantiate is called (executed) that serves as a way to make copies of any object in a scene. The Instantiate function requires three pieces of information, or arguments, to do its job: the object to be copied, the new position for the copy and its rotation. These three arguments are between the opening and closing parentheses after Instantiate, separated by commas. The first of these values is gameObject which refers to the current object, in this case the cube. Then new_position adds the location that should be given to the copy. Finally, Quaternion.identity represents how much to rotate the new cube, in this case not at all. A quaternion is similar to a vector in that it holds a list of numbers, but instead of three it holds four: three numbers that establish an axis, or direction, and one that specifies the degree of rotation around that axis.

Fig. 1.10 The rotating cubes example in action.

The information presented so far touches on just a few of the many capabilities of Unity. Although basic, knowing your way around the interface, being able to position objects in a scene and some familiarity with adding behaviors through scripting are essential skills needed to move forward. I recommend rereading any pieces in this chapter that seem unclear so the more complex work ahead is easier to comprehend. Remember as well that the

Support section of the Unity website has a lot of information that can clarify concepts in a complementary way to the instruction provided in this book. The wealth of knowledge there should serve as a companion reference and I will point out particular resources throughout.

In the following chapters I will be guiding you through a wide range of what is possible with Unity. I will dig deeper into some of the aspects presented above such as the variables, functions and calculations that go into scripting. I will also be exploring many new capabilities like physics simulation, animation, graphic effects, interactivity and lighting. With each example design game I will discuss the design task under consideration and how that task gets translated into working software. Learning the ins and outs of working with Unity is certainly one outcome, but the primary goal is to explore a method of design thinking in which analyzing processes and encoding them into playful tools opens up new possibilities and potentials. It is just as much about gaining new insights into the process of design as it is about learning new and valuable techniques.

The companion website for this book has additional resources that are essential for getting the most out of the chapters that follow. Before proceeding on, pay a visit to it:

 www.routledge.com/cw/westre

There are more tips and techniques on the site as well as discussions of topics that didn't fit into the book. The most important thing to do on the site is to download the resources package and take a look inside. It contains starter and finished projects for each of the example design games. These resources will accelerate your progress as you work through each of the exercises. Once you have everything, you're ready to dive into creating your own design games.

2

BUILDING BLOCKS

2.1 · The Brief

Pat is a designer looking for a tool to use for short periods of time throughout the day to spark some creative energy. His idea is to have something akin to a set of children's building blocks. It would be a kind of toy that would allow him to explore 3D forms, or to simply take a break from work while still flexing some creative muscle. Pat doesn't want something that behaves exactly like blocks. Instead, his desire is for something more game-like that would be simple to use, but produce somewhat unpredictable results. He feels like a playful, unpredictable design game could offer him a tool for getting 'unstuck' when encountering creative roadblocks. Your job in this chapter is to create a design game for Pat that fits these requirements.

2.2 · The Proposal

Though Pat's requirements above offer some idea about the type of design game he wants, there are still several aspects of the design game left unresolved. The most important question is how to make a set of virtual blocks that encourages unpredictable results. There are several techniques found commonly in video games that could be useful here. Randomization is an easy choice. By determining the number, size or placement of the blocks based on random values the outcome would be, by definition, quite unpredictable. A time limit might be useful as well. Setting a fast-approaching deadline for a task can lend a sense of urgency to the block stacking. The logic of how the blocks get stacked is another aspect that can be altered. Though somewhat counterintuitive, constraining the manner in which the blocks are assembled can improve the chances of arriving at interesting forms.

There are many ways to combine randomness, time limits and constraints into a set of rules for an interesting design game, but they need to be balanced. If there is too much randomness, it will feel nonsensical. If the time limit is too short, the designer won't be able to assemble very complex or interesting forms. If the placement of the blocks is too constrained, the same arrangements will keep appearing over and over. On the other hand, if the rules lack enough constraints, the design game could seem too open-ended, leaving the designer with no sense of direction.

Luckily the video game world is full of elegant solutions that combine these elements in a ratio that yields unpredictable results while keeping the game play simple and fun. Since the activity here is stacking blocks, an appropriate example is the game Tetris. In Tetris, a player arranges falling blocks so that they fit together to fill horizontal rows on the game board, thereby eliminating rows of blocks. Blocks of different shapes appear at the top of the screen that are randomly determined. As the block falls down the screen, the player can move it right or left and rotate it 90 degrees at a time. They can speed up the block's fall, but not slow it down. If the blocks pile up to the top of the screen, the game is lost. This imposes a kind of adaptive time limit – the better a player is at arranging solid rows, the longer they play.

For this design game, Tetris can serve as a productive starting point for determining a well-balanced set of rules. A 3D version, in which random blocks fall and can be positioned by the designer, seems to fit the design task quite well. In the interest of keeping the design game simple, the variety of sizes of the blocks will be limited to four.

One of these four blocks, determined randomly, will appear and start to fall. The designer will be able to move and rotate the falling block by using the keyboard. Once the block comes to rest on the game board, or on another block, a new block starts falling. In order to limit the length of each session, when the designer stacks their blocks higher than 10 units, the current session will end. The designer will have a chance to review the form they produced, then start a new one if they desire.

Why build a version of Tetris? When building your first design game, it can be quite helpful to start with a well-known example. The game play of Tetris is simple and it can serve as an easy-to-understand template. In subsequent chapters, the projects will roam further afield, incorporating more complex techniques.

2.3 · Opening the Project

For this and each of the following design game examples, I've provided a finished version of the Unity project along with a starter project. A 'project' in Unity is a folder that contains all of the pieces of a game on which you are working. You can find the example project files in the resources package on the companion website. The starter projects have some pre-assembled pieces to allow for clearer instruction and faster progress as the examples grow in complexity. Feel free to open the finished examples at any time as you complete the exercises in this book. Looking at the finished projects can help clarify steps you may be confused about. Grab the code at:

www.routledge.com/cw/westre

You can find the starter project for this chapter, called BuildingBlocksStarter, Building Blocks folder. To open the project, start up Unity and select **File > Open Project** from the main menu. In the Project Wizard window, click the Open Other button. The Choose Project Directory window should appear; here you can select the BuildingBlocksStarter folder.

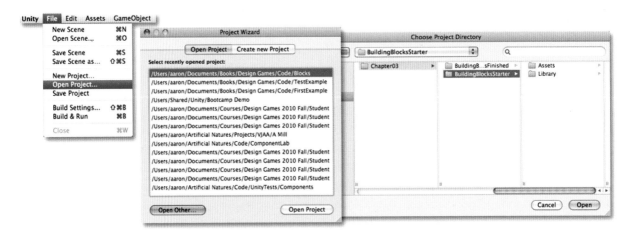

Fig. 2.1 Opening the BuildingBlocksStarter project.

When opening an existing project, sometimes a new untitled scene is created. If this is the case you will see a blank Scene View and the word 'Untitled' at the top of the Unity window. Instead of using this scene, open the MainScene by double-clicking it in the Project View. In the Scene View you should see a few objects that I've created to help you get started.

There are four objects in this scene called Main Camera, Directional light, GameBoard and Guide. Take a look at each of these objects by clicking on them in the Hierarchy. Whenever an object is highlighted in the Hierarchy, it is also highlighted in the Scene View and its parameters are displayed in the Inspector. If you highlight the Main Camera, you'll see that I've set the position and rotation so that it overlooks the GameBoard. The Directional light has been positioned as well, to cast light on the scene at a slight angle. Highlighting the GameBoard reveals that it is a cube that has been scaled to 20 units along the x and z axes so that it forms a large, flat square. This is where the blocks will fall when the design game is being played. The GameBoard has been covered with a grid pattern to give the

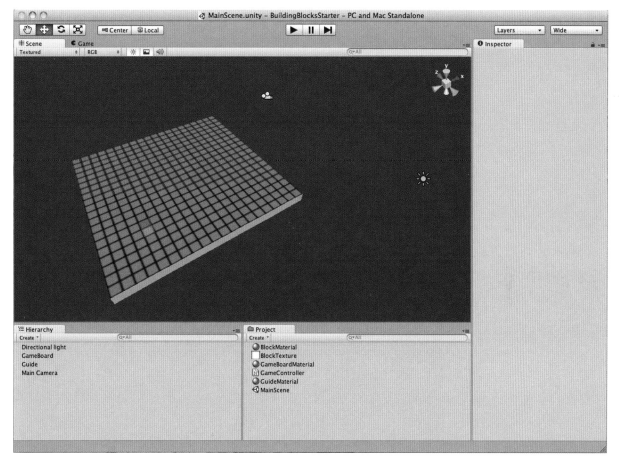

Fig. 2.2 The BuildingBlocksStarter project, with the MainScene open.

player a clearer notion of where blocks will land. The last object in the scene is called Guide. It is a cube that has a material which gives it a semi-transparent orange tint. The purpose of this object will become clear as you build the project.

2.4 · Prefab

Place a cube in the scene by selecting **GameObject > Create Other > Cube** from the main menu. You can also create a cube, and many other objects, using the Create menu in the Hierarchy. When a new object is created, it is placed in the scene so that it appears in the center of the Scene View. This means that its position will be some arbitrary point that may or may not be desirable. To fit the needs of this project, the cube will need to be placed at the origin (0, 0, 0). Do this by setting the x, y and z values of the cube's position to zero in the Inspector. The cube will move to a point in the middle of the GameBoard.

To give the cube a bit more definition, you can apply a material to it. Materials are used to add colors, textures and other effects to the surface of objects. In the Project View there is a material called BlockMaterial. Drag and drop this onto the cube in the Hierarchy. This will cover the cube in the same texture that forms the grid on the GameBoard. It will improve the visibility of the blocks when the design game is being played. To see this change more clearly, highlight the cube in the Hierarchy and, with the mouse cursor inside the Scene View, press the F key. This will zoom in so that the cube fills the Scene View. To zoom back out, scroll back using the mouse or hold down the Control key and drag.

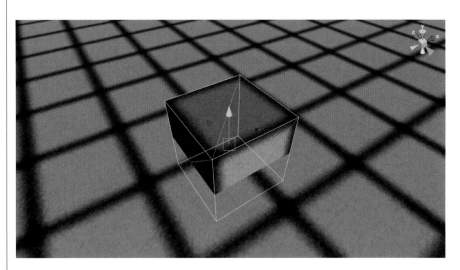

Fig. 2.3 The Scene View zoomed in to see the block.

The Building Blocks design game is supposed to have four different sizes of blocks to ensure that the forms created are unpredictable. There are many different ways to achieve this variety. You could create four cubes of various scales (proportional dimensions) to serve as the blocks. Alternatively, you could assemble larger blocks using standard 1 unit cubes. This project will employ the simpler technique of making copies of the cube you just created and scaling those copies to one of four sizes. To do this, the cube needs to be turned into an object called a prefab. You can think of prefabs as templates from which new objects can be created. Select **Assets > Create > Prefab** from the main menu or by selecting Prefab from the Create menu in the Project View. An item called New Prefab will appear in the Project View. Rename this prefab by clicking on it once and typing the name Block. The final step is to drag and drop the Cube from the Hierarchy onto the Block prefab. The cube icon next to the Block will turn blue to indicate that it is now usable. The Block prefab will be the template from which all the blocks will be created. With the prefab complete, the cube is no longer necessary. To remove it from the scene, right-click on the Cube in the Hierarchy and select Delete.

Fig. 2.4 Deleting the cube.

2.5 · Defining Variables

Creating copies of the Block prefab requires some code. There is a script called GameController provided in the Project View. This script will contain all the code necessary to run the design game. If you highlight the script in the Project View, you'll see that there are a number of variables (lines starting with var) and functions (starting with function). These pieces will serve as a structure in which the rules of the design game will be defined. In order for this script to operate it needs to be attached to an object in the scene. Since every scene contains a camera, named Main Camera, this is usually a good object to attach a script to, like this one, that will control the action of a game. Attach the script to the camera by dragging and dropping GameController from the Project View onto the Main Camera in the Hierarchy. By highlighting the Main Camera you can see that the script is now listed along with the other components in the Inspector. Double-clicking the GameController script in the Project View will open it in the MonoDevelop editor. MonoDevelop is a text editor that is included with Unity for the purpose of writing Unity scripts. With the GameController script open in MonoDevelop, take a look at the variables at the top of the script.

Learn more about scripts and variables in the Chapter 2 section of the companion website.

Listing 2.1 Variable definitions.

```
var game_board : GameObject;
var block_prefab : GameObject;
var guide : GameObject;
var current_block : GameObject;
var next_block : GameObject;

var cam_pos_1 : Vector3;
var cam_pos_2 : Vector3;
var cam_pos_3 : Vector3;
var start_point : Vector3;
var next_point : Vector3;
```

```
var start_rotation : Quaternion;

var time_step : float;
var next_step : float;
var falling_step : float;
var move_step : float;

var paused : boolean;
var game_over : boolean;
```

These lines are called variable definitions. The var keyword establishes that this line serves to define a variable or reference to some value. The next word is the name of the variable. Variable names cannot contain spaces or punctuation except the underscore character (_). The first variable above could be called game_board or GameBoard, but not Game board. I'm using underscores to separate words in variable names to improve readability, but there are many other naming conventions that are used. The colon (:) can be read as 'is of type' and what follows is the type of the variable being defined. The semicolon (;) signifies the end of the definition.

There are several different types assigned to the variables in the code above. GameObject refers to an object in the scene or Project View. Vector3 refers to x, y and z coordinates. Quaternion encodes a rotation. A float represents a floating point, or number with a factional component (as opposed to int which refers to whole numbers). A boolean can be either true or false. Specifying the type of a variable is optional. The definitions above could have been written 'var variable_name;' while still functioning. However making sure these variables have types protects against errors that could occur if the wrong type of value is assigned. Specifying type also allows the variables to be set more easily in the Inspector. To see this in action, highlight the Main Camera in the Hierarchy and look at the variables under the GameController script.

Here values can be assigned to each variable without having to do so in the script. This can save time by reducing the amount of code that needs to be written and can make changing the values of variables much simpler. These variables need to be assigned before the rest of the code can be written. The first five variables listed in the Inspector are of the type GameObject. They will refer to the objects of which the rest of the script will make use. To start, assign the Game_board variable by dragging and dropping the GameBoard from the Hierarchy onto the Game_board line in the Inspector. This can

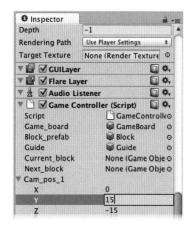

Fig. 2.5 Assigning values to variables in the Inspector (shown here in three parts).

be a bit tricky to do initially, since it's easy to highlight the object being dragged, changing what the Inspector is displaying. The key is not to highlight the GameBoard in the Hierarchy but to click, hold and drag it over to the Inspector. Using the same technique, drag Block from the Project View onto the Block_prefab line and Guide from the Hierarchy onto the line that reads Guide. The Current_block and Next_block lines can be left as none.

The five variables following the GameObject variables are of the type Vector3. Clicking on the triangle to the left of the variable name will reveal the x, y and z values of the vector. Set Cam_pos_1 to (0, 15, −15), Cam_pos_2 to (0, 20, 0) and Cam_pos_3 to (−15, 15, −15). Start_point and Next_point should be set to (0, 10.5, 0) and (−5, 10.5, 0) respectively. Leaving Start_rotation at its defaults (all zeros), the following four variables are floating point numbers. Set Time_step to 0.5, Next_step to 0, Falling_step and Move_step to 1. Paused and Game_over, boolean variables, can be left unchecked (false).

2.6 · Adding Functionality

With these variables assigned, you can start to add functionality to the design game. Open the GameController script or return to the script editor window. Find the CreateBlock function and write code so it looks like the listing shown here.

Listing 2.2 CreateBlock function.

```
function CreateBlock ()
{
```

```
    var new_block = Instantiate(block_prefab,
                                next_point,
                                start_rotation);
    return new_block;
}
```

The first line inside the CreateBlock function creates a variable called new_block and sets it equal to the results of a function called Instantiate. As you learned in the previous chapter, Instantiate creates copies of objects. It needs three arguments, or pieces of information, to do its job: the object to copy, the position and the rotation. These arguments are supplied as block_prefab, next_point and start_rotation, three variables that you set up in the Inspector. The block_prefab refers to the cube that was converted to the prefab called Block. The next_point and start_rotation specify that the copy of the Block prefab should be placed above the GameBoard with no rotation. I've placed next_point and start_rotation on separate lines in the code for formatting reasons. The statement starting with var new_block and ending at the semicolon can all be placed on the same line, as long as the commas separate the arguments inside the parentheses. It works either way since whitespace – spaces, tabs and newlines – doesn't really matter in JavaScript. In fact, entire scripts can be written all on a single line though typically whitespace is used to make the code more readable. The last line inside the CreateBlock function returns, or hands back, a reference to the new_block variable. The reason for this will become clear in the next step.

Locate the Start function and add the following code.

Listing 2.3 Start function.

```
function Start ()
{
    current_block = CreateBlock();
    current_block.transform.position = start_point;
    next_block = CreateBlock();
    next_step = Time.time + time_step;
}
```

The Start function serves a special purpose. The instructions inside are carried out only once, when the game first starts up. It's useful for setting up initial conditions. Here two variables, current_block and next_block, which have been defined, but not assigned, are given values. Recall the

CreateBlock function you wrote. It makes a copy of the Block prefab, scales it and returns – or sends back – a reference to that copy. Here in the Start function, CreateBlock is called twice to make two new blocks. The variables current_block and next_block are used to store references to those blocks.

When these blocks are produced in the CreateBlock function, they are positioned at a point referred to by the next_point variable. You assigned the point (−5, 10.5, 0) to this variable, meaning the new blocks will appear above the GameBoard and a bit to the left of its center. On the second line inside the curly braces, the position of current_block is set to the variable start_point which was set to 10.5 units above the center of the GameBoard. From here, it is ready to begin its fall downward. Having these two copies means that as the player moves the falling block, they will be able to see which block is on deck.

The last line in the Start function sets the next_step variable equal to the current time (Time.time) plus time_step which was set to 0.5, or half a second. The next_step variable will be used to keep track of when blocks should fall towards the GameBoard.

2.7 · Falling

Now that two Block copies have been created, they need to fall. The code for this gets added to the Update function.

Listing 2.4 Update function.

```
function Update ()
{
    if (paused)
    {
        next_step = Time.time;
    } else {
        if (Time.time > next_step)
        {
            next_step = Time.time + time_step;
            current_block.transform.position.y -=
falling_step;
        }
    }
    if (Input.GetKeyUp(KeyCode.Space))
    {
```

```
        paused = !paused;
    }
}
```

Recall from the previous chapter that code inside the Update function gets executed during every frame when the design game is running. This happens 30 to 60 times per second or more depending on computer hardware. Inside this function there are several blocks of code called if statements. An if statement is a way to execute different sets of instructions depending on what's going on in the game. The basic structure looks like the following.

Listing 2.5 The basic structure of an if statement.

```
if (statement to evaluate)
{
    code to run if statement is true...
} else {
    code to run if statement is false...
}
```

Learn more about if statements in the Chapter 2 section of the companion website.

If the statement to evaluate turns out to be true, then the code inside the first set of curly braces is executed. If it's false, then the second section, following the word else, is executed.

Take a look at the bottom of the Update function. There is an if statement that allows the player to pause the game using the space bar. This is accomplished by setting a variable named 'paused' to true or false. It tests for whether the space bar has been pressed by using the function Input.GetKeyUp. The Input.GetKeyUp function can test whether any key on the keyboard has been pressed and released during the current frame. If the space bar has been pressed, then the line 'paused = !paused' is executed. The exclamation point (!) means 'not', so this line reads 'set paused equal to the opposite of paused'. This is a way of switching the paused variable back and forth from true to false.

The first if statement in the Update function tests for whether the variable paused is true or false. At this point paused is equal to false which means the instructions in the else section will be carried out. Inside that else block is another if statement that determines whether the current block should fall down one step. Time.time refers to the current time and next_step refers to the time at which the falling block should make its next plunge downward.

This has the effect of moving the block downward in increments every half second (the value of time_step). So, if it is true that the current time is equal or later than (>=) the scheduled time for the next move, the code inside gets executed. This code does two things. First, `next_step` is updated so that the next move is scheduled at a half second in the future (`Time.time + time_step`). Then the block referred to by current_block is lowered by one unit, the value to which `falling_step` is set.

Back up at the top of the Update function, if the paused variable is true, the next_step variable is set to the current time. Since this is the only instruction carried out if paused is true, the current block won't fall. When paused is set to false, the next_step variable will be set to the current time and the current block will start falling again immediately.

Take a moment to save the script and click the play button to start the design game running. You should see a block falling. As the block falls press the space bar to pause the game. This should stop the current block from falling. The current block falls like the pieces in Tetris fall: in halting increments. The first of the functionality of the design game is now in place.

What went wrong?
If you are having problems getting the code to work, see the Chapter 2 section of the companion website for some tips.

2.8 · Moving the Block

The player needs to be able to move the block around and rotate it in order to create forms. Arrow keys on the keyboard will be a straightforward way to control the movement of the block left, right, forward and back as it is falling. The R key will be used to rotate the block 90 degrees at a time. Start by locating the MoveBlock function in the GameController script and typing in the following code.

Listing 2.6 The MoveBlock function.

```
function MoveBlock(dir : String)
{
    var cb_position = current_block.transform.position;
    var cb_rotation = current_block.transform.rotation;
    if (dir == "right")
    {
        current_block.transform.position.x += move_step;
    } else if (dir == "left") {
        current_block.transform.position.x -= move_step;
    } else if (dir == "up") {
        current_block.transform.position.z += move_step;
```

```
    } else if (dir == "down") {
        current_block.transform.position.z -= move_step;
    } else if (dir == "rotate") {
        current_block.transform.Rotate(Vector3.up * 90);
    }
    var limits = Bounds(Vector3(0, 5.5, 0), Vector3(20, 10, 20));
    var cb_bounds = current_block.GetComponent(Renderer).bounds;
    if ( !limits.Contains(cb_bounds.min) ||
         !limits.Contains(cb_bounds.max) )
    {
        current_block.transform.position = cb_position;
        current_block.transform.rotation = cb_rotation;
    }
}

function MoveBlock(dir : String)
{
    var cb_position = current_block.transform.position;
    var cb_rotation = current_block.transform.rotation;
    if (dir == "right")
    {
        current_block.transform.position.x += move_step;
    } else if (dir == "left") {
        current_block.transform.position.x -= move_step;
    } else if (dir == "up") {
        current_block.transform.position.z += move_step;
    } else if (dir == "down") {
        current_block.transform.position.z -= move_step;
    } else if (dir == "rotate") {
        current_block.transform.Rotate(Vector3.up * 90);
    }
    var limits = Bounds(Vector3(0, 5.5, 0), Vector3(20, 10, 20));
    var cb_bounds = current_block.GetComponent(Renderer).bounds;
    if ( !limits.Contains(cb_bounds.min) ||
         !limits.Contains(cb_bounds.max) )
    {
        current_block.transform.position = cb_position;
        current_block.transform.rotation = cb_rotation;
    }
}
```

In the very top line you can see that, in the parentheses following
MoveBlock, this function requires one argument, named dir. This piece of

information is of type String, as evinced by the ' : String' following the argument name dir. This means that to call this function – to cause it to carry out its instructions – a string, or piece of text, must be provided. That text will specify what direction the block should be moved in, e.g. MoveBlock("right") to move to the right, or positive x direction.

At a basic level, this function records the current position and rotation of the block. Then it moves or rotates the block according to the text argument called dir. Finally it determines whether the block is still within the limits of the GameBoard and, if it's not, reverses any action taken. This way the block can't be moved such that it floats off into empty space. It adds a constraint to the design game that requires each block to be positioned over the GameBoard.

The first two lines of code inside the MoveBlock function do the job of recording the block's current placement. The variables `cb_position` and `cb_rotation` are set equal to the position and rotation of the block that is falling, referred to by the `current_block` variable. Next there is an if statement that looks slightly different than those you've written so far. The first line of this statement – `if (dir == "right")` – makes use of a special symbol, the double equal sign. This symbol can be read as 'is equal to'. It's different than the single equal sign in that it tests for equality between two values, whereas the single equal sign assigns a value to a variable. So, in the first line, the if statement is testing whether the argument dir is equal to the string "right". If this is true, the block is moved along the positive x axis by the value referred to by the variable `move_step`, which you have set to one. What follows are four 'else if' blocks. These test for whether the block should move left, up, down or should be rotated. The phrase 'else if', followed by an evaluation in parentheses, is a way to chain together related tests into a single if statement. It's typically used when only one of a set of conditions can happen. In each of the first four sections of the if statement, the position of the falling block is added to or subtracted from using the += and -= symbols. The symbols, like the equal sign, are called assignment operators in that they alter the value referred to by a variable. The += can be read as 'is increased by' and -= as 'is decreased by'. If you wanted to increase the value of a variable called some_number by one, you could write 'some_number = some_number + 1;'. The += and -= operators offer a shortcut such that the preceding assignment statement can be written as 'some_number += 1;'. The final else if in the if statement applies a rotation to the block. This is done via the `Rotate` function that is a part of the transform component of each object in a scene.

To achieve a specific rotation, the Rotate function needs a vector multiplied by an angle in degrees. Here, `Vector3.up` represents the direction pointing along the positive y axis and 90 represents 90 degrees positive (clockwise looking from above) degrees.

In programming terminology, a collection of data and functions is known as an object. There are visible objects in a scene, such as your block, that contain data, like position, geometry and appearance. In addition, there are also invisible objects that don't show up in the scene, but instead serve as references to some useful set of data. One of these is a Bounds object. Bounds objects are made up of two vectors, one describing a center point and one defining the overall size. Essentially it's an imaginary cube that has some handy capabilities, like testing whether a point is inside its bounds. The variable named 'limits', a Bounds object, refers to an imaginary cube positioned over the GameBoard that constrains where the blocks can travel. The last few lines of code in the MoveBlock function determine whether the falling block has moved outside the area of play defined by limits and, if so, moves the block back to where it was.

Recall that there are two variables, cb_position and cb_rotation, that record the original placement of the falling block named current_block. After limits has been assigned its value, the next line defines a variable named `cb_bounds` that refers to a Bounds object, like limits. It represents the outer boundary of current_block. The if statement that follows uses limits in conjunction with cb_bounds to determine whether any point on current_block has moved outside the bounds defined by limits.

Listing 2.7 The if statement testing if current_block has moved outside of limits.

```
...
    if ( !limits.Contains(cb_bounds.min) ||
         !limits.Contains(cb_bounds.max) )
    {
        current_block.transform.position = cb_position;
        current_block.transform.rotation = cb_rotation;
    }
...
```

On the first line of this code, within the parentheses, are two tests separated by a double pipe symbol (||). The double pipe symbol stands for the word 'or'. If either of the tests is true, then the code inside the if statement will be executed. The two tests use a function named `Contains` that is part of every Bounds object. The Contains function determines whether a point lies within the boundary of the Bounds object. If it does, the test is true, and if not, it's false. The points that are given to the Contains function are parameters of a Bounds object called `min` and `max`. They refer to the numerically smallest and largest points, or corners, of the boundary. Here, the min and max points given are those of current_block. Geometrically speaking, if either of these points lies outside the limits boundary, the block should be moved back to its previous location. The two lines inside the if statement return the block to the previous position and rotation, if necessary, using the cb_position and cb_rotation variables respectively.

To reiterate, the MoveBlock function performs three distinct actions. First, it stores the position and rotation of current_block. Then, the block is moved or rotated according to the dir argument. Last, two sets of bounds are used to determine whether the falling block has moved outside the limits and, if so, repositions the block to its former location.

In order for the MoveBlock function to do its job, a few lines of code need to be added to the Update function. Read over the code below and try to determine how the five new if statements work. Then locate the Update function in the GameController script again and insert the code as shown below.

Listing 2.8 An updated Update function (previous code in gray).

```
function Update ()
{
    if (paused)
    {
        next_step = Time.time;
    } else {
        if (Time.time > next_step)
        {
            next_step += time_step;
            next_step = Time.time + time_step;
            current_block.transform.position.y -= falling_step;
        }
        if (Input.GetKeyUp("r"))
        {
            MoveBlock("rotate");
        }
        if (Input.GetKeyUp(KeyCode.RightArrow))
```

```
          {
              MoveBlock("right");
          }
          if (Input.GetKeyUp(KeyCode.LeftArrow))
          {
              MoveBlock("left");
          }
          if (Input.GetKeyUp(KeyCode.UpArrow))
          {
              MoveBlock("up");
          }
          if (Input.GetKeyUp(KeyCode.DownArrow))
          {
              MoveBlock("down");
          }
      }
      if (Input.GetKeyUp(KeyCode.Space))
      {
          paused = !paused;
      }
  }
}
```

In each of the new if statements, the `Input.GetKeyUp` function is used to test whether the R key ("r") or any of the arrow keys (KeyCode.RightArrow, etc.) have been pressed during the current frame. In each case the MoveBlock function is executed and passed the appropriate message to trigger the desired movement.

Save the GameController script and play the design game. Test whether the falling block does indeed stay within bounds by pressing the arrow and R keys. The range of movement should be restricted to the area over the GameBoard.

2.9 · Touch Down

Moving and rotating the block now works, but it still falls straight through the GameBoard. To fix this, some logic needs to be in place that stops the block once it touches the surface of the GameBoard. Since there will be multiple blocks that should stack on top of each other, there also needs to be a way to determine if one block has landed on top of another. You can add both of these capabilities to the HasTouchedDown function in the GameController script by adding the code below.

Listing 2.9 The HasTouchedDown function.

```
function HasTouchedDown ()
{
    var current_y = current_block.transform.position.y - 0.5;
    if (current_y <= 0)
    {
        return true;
    } else {
        var cb_bounds = current_block.GetComponent(Renderer).
bounds;
        cb_bounds.Expand( Vector3(-0.1, 0, -0.1) );
        var landed_blocks =
            GameObject.FindGameObjectsWithTag("Landed");
        for (var landed_block in landed_blocks)
        {
            var b_bounds =
                landed_block.GetComponent(Renderer).bounds;
            if (b_bounds.Intersects(cb_bounds))
            {
                return true;
            }
        }
        return false;
    }
}
```

Basically the code in this function says if the falling block has touched the GameBoard, return true, meaning 'confirm that the block has touched down'. If the block hasn't touched the GameBoard, a test is run to see if it has touched any of the blocks that have already landed and, if so, it returns true. If the block hasn't touched any objects in the scene, the function returns false and the block continues to fall.

The current_y variable is set to the distance between the bottom of the falling block and the GameBoard. In Unity, every object's position is located at its center. Since all of the blocks will be one unit deep, 0.5 is subtracted to specify the height of the bottom surface of the block.

The if statement that follows tests whether the bottom surface of the block (current_y) has reached the top surface of the GameBoard (at y = 0). The <= symbol used here can be read as 'is less than or equal to'. If the bottom of the block is at zero then the function returns true. If the block hasn't touched the GameBoard, then the code inside the else section goes into effect.

Inside the else section, the first line defines a variable called `landed_blocks`. It's a type of variable, known as an array, that refers to a list of items. The `GameObject.FindGameObjectsWithTag` function searches through the scene and returns an array of all of the objects that have been tagged with a specific word. Here the tag is "Landed", which has been set up specifically for this project. A tag serves as a way to label objects so they can be found easily. Tags can be defined in the Inspector to label objects and later retrieve them using code.

Now that there is a list of all of the blocks that have landed on the GameBoard, or on another block, each one can be tested to determine if the falling block has touched down. This is done using a 'for loop', which is a type of statement known as an iterator. A for loop iterates through each item in an array one by one until it reaches the end of the list. The line 'for `(var landed_block in landed_blocks)`' sets up a variable named `landed_block` that will refer to the current item in the landed_blocks array as the for loop goes through the list.

Inside the curly braces of the for loop, a variable named `cb_bounds` is set up, which should be familiar to you from the MoveBlock function. It corresponds to the boundary of the falling block. On the next line, another Bounds object named `b_bounds` is set to the bounds of landed_block, the current item in the landed_blocks array being iterated through. Then an if statement tests whether these bounds are touching the bounds of the falling block. All Bounds objects have a function named `Intersects` which can be used to determine this. If the Intersects function finds that the two blocks are touching, the function returns true and stops executing. If the for loop goes through all of the landed blocks and hasn't returned true, the line following the for loop causes the function to return false and stops executing. The HasTouchedDown function will be used to determine when to stop the current block from falling when it has touched the GameBoard, or another block.

In order to have the HasTouchedDown function do its work, some more logic needs to be added to the Update method. The following code listing shows only an excerpt of the Update function to save space, but gives enough context to show you where to place the new code.

Learn more about loops in the Chapter 2 section of the companion website.

Listing 2.10 An excerpt of the Update method (new code in black).

```
...
if (Time.time > next_step)
```

```
{
    next_step += time_step;
    next_step = Time.time + time_step;
    if (HasTouchedDown())
    {
        current_block.tag = "Landed";
        current_block = next_block;
        current_block.transform.position = start_point;
        next_block = CreateBlock();
    } else {
        current_block.transform.position.y -= falling_step;
    }
}
if (Input.GetKeyUp("r"))
{
    MoveBlock("rotate");
}
...
```

An if statement has been added that executes the HasTouchedDown function to see if the falling block should be stopped. If the falling block hasn't touched down, it continues to fall as it did before, using the line inside the else section of the statement. However, if the falling block has touched either the GameBoard or another block, the code inside performs a few tasks. First the falling block is tagged with the word "Landed" so it can be identified in the future. Then the current_block variable is set to refer to the block that is on deck, named next_block. The new current block is then moved into the starting position. Finally, the next_block variable is assigned a new copy of the Block prefab.

Save the GameController script and click the play button. The falling block should now stop when it reaches the GameBoard. Once the first block touches down, a new block will start its descent. If you allow a few blocks to fall without moving them, they should begin to stack up. Take a well-deserved break from writing code. Play the game a few times, stacking the blocks up in various ways. Do you recognize a problem?

Listing 2.11 Shrinking the bounds of the falling block in the HasTouchedDown function.

```
...
    } else {
        var cb_bounds = current_block.GetComponent(Renderer).bounds;
```

```
cb_bounds.Expand( Vector3(-0.1, 0, -0.1) );
var landed_blocks =
     GameObject.FindGameObjectsWithTag("Landed");
```

. . .

When the falling block touches a side, other than the top, of a block that has already landed, it can stop without coming to rest on top of the GameBoard or another block. Anyone who's played Tetris knows that blocks should be able to slide past each other. What is going on here?

The solution to this problem lies in the HasTouchedDown function. The Intersects function is used to determine whether the bounds of the falling block are intersecting the bounds of any of the landed blocks. The Intersects function doesn't determine how bounds are intersecting, only if they are. Thus, when blocks are touching at their sides, this function returns true, just as it does if the blocks are stacked vertically.

A new line of code added to the HasTouchedDown function allows the falling block to slide past other blocks. All Bounds objects have a function named Expand. This function counterintuitively shrinks the size of those bounds. The Expand function takes a vector as an argument that specifies by how much it should be expanded along each of its three dimensions. By using negative numbers for the x and z values in Vector3 (–0.1, 0, –0.1), the bounds of the block are reduced along those axes. This allows the falling block to slide past other blocks even if their sides are touching.

Click play again to verify that blocks are stacking up properly. There should be no blocks that stop when they are not stacked directly on top of the GameBoard or another block. Once this is working, you're well on your way to a fully functioning design game.

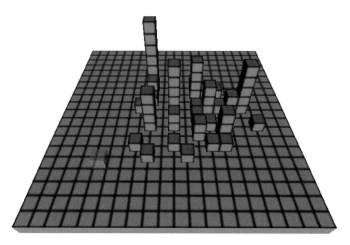

Fig. 2.6 Blocks stacking up.

2.10 · A Bit of Randomness

At the beginning of this chapter, the requirements of this design game called for four different sizes of blocks. This can be accomplished by introducing some random variation into the code.

Listing 2.12 Revised CreateBlock function (new code in black).

```
function CreateBlock ()
{
    var new_block = Instantiate(block_prefab,
                            next_point,
                            start_rotation);
    var new_size;
    var rand = Random.value;
    if (rand < 0.25)
    {
        new_size = Vector3(2.0, 1.0, 2.0);
    } else if (rand >= 0.25 && rand < 0.5) {
        new_size = Vector3(4.0, 1.0, 2.0);
    } else if (rand >= 0.5 && rand < 0.75) {
        new_size = Vector3(4.0, 1.0, 4.0);
    } else {
        new_size = Vector3(6.0, 1.0, 2.0);
    }
    new_block.transform.localScale = new_size;
    return new_block;
}
```

On the first new line, a variable named `new_size` is declared. The verb declare, in this context, is a programming term that means to name a variable, but not to assign a value to it. The new_size variable will later refer to a vector with the dimensions of the new block being created. On the next line a variable named `rand` is set to a random number between 0 and 1. `Random. value` is a constantly shifting floating point number. Each time it's used it refers to a new random value. The if statement here determines which size the new block will be, based on the value of rand.

Read the code above and see if you can figure out how the sizes of the four blocks are being determined.

Two questions may arise: what does `&&` mean and how do the three numbers after Vector3 encode the size of a block? The double ampersand symbol (`&&`) in the middle can be read as 'and', meaning both of the tests in parentheses need to be true for the code in that section to be executed. The three numbers in a vector correspond to the three axes: x, y and z. A vector can encode a point in space or a direction, but here the x, y and z values correspond to the number of units that the new block will have along each axis. As mentioned previously, all blocks in this game are one unit tall.

For example if rand is 0.3, it is both greater than or equal to (>=) 0.25 and less than (<) 0.5, so new_size is assigned a vector of four by one by two units. If rand is 0.75 or greater, then the code in the last else section sets new_size to six by one by two units. An else if isn't needed here, since this is the only remaining result. Finally, the size of the new block is set to match the new_size variable.

Play the design game to get a feel for how these new randomly sized blocks work. Be sure to move the blocks around and rotate them as they fall. See what kinds of forms you can create.

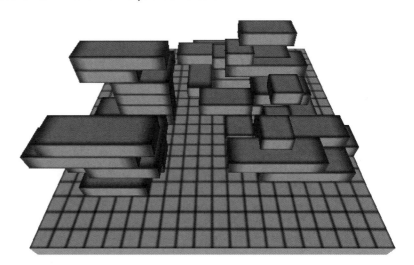

Fig. 2.7 Stacks of multi-sized blocks.

2.11 · Guides and Views

You may have noticed that, at times, it's rather difficult to figure out where a block is going to land. In two-dimensional games like Tetris, moving a block precisely into position is relatively simple. However, the camera in this design game is showing a perspectival view of a three-dimensional scene. In this type of view, objects in the foreground block your view of objects in the background. Next you will add two elements to Building Blocks that will make guiding blocks much easier to understand in this 3D environment. The first of these elements is a guide that will indicate to the player where on the GameBoard the falling block will land. Add the following code to the DrawGuide function in the GameController script.

Listing 2.13 The DrawGuide function.

```
function DrawGuide ()
{
    var cb_pos = current_block.transform.position;
    var cb_scale = current_block.transform.localScale;
    var cb_rot = current_block.transform.rotation;
    guide.transform.position = Vector3( cb_pos.x,
                                        (cb_pos.y / 2) - 0.5,
                                        cb_pos.z );
    guide.transform.localScale = Vector3( cb_scale.x,
                                           cb_pos.y,
                                           cb_scale.z );
    guide.transform.rotation = cb_rot;
}
```

If you've been wondering about the purpose of the mysterious, translucent orange cube in the scene, now you will finally see it in action. In the 'Defining Variables' section, you assigned this cube to the variable named guide. The DrawGuide function positions the orange guide cube between the falling block and the GameBoard. It will form a column descending from the falling block, indicating where it will land.

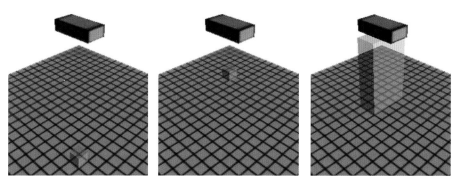
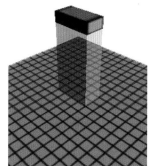

Fig. 2.8 From left to right: The guide in its original location, positioned halfway between the block and GameBoard, scaled to size and rotated to match the block.

The first three variables defined in the function – cb_pos, cb_scale and cb_rot – record the position, scale and rotation of the current_block. The position of the guide (guide.transform.position) is set to the same x and z values as current_block, but a y value that is halfway between the bottom surface of that block and the top surface of the GameBoard. The expression (cb_pos.y / 2) - 0.5 gives this y value. Recall that a Unity object is always positioned using its center point. Placing the guide halfway between the current block and the GameBoard will allow it to be resized.

Next, the scale of the guide (guide.transform.localScale) is set equal to the x and z dimensions of current_block. To fill all of the space it needs to, the y dimension of the guide is set equal to the y position of current_block which is the distance from the GameBoard to the block. Last, the rotation of the guide is set to match the rotation of current_block. For square blocks this doesn't really matter, but it's necessary in order for the guide to be in alignment with rectangular blocks. Now one line needs to be added to the Update function, as shown below.

Listing 2.14 An excerpt of the Update function, showing DrawGuide(); on the last line.

```
. . .
    if (Input.GetKeyUp(KeyCode.Space))
    {
        paused = !paused;
    }
    DrawGuide();
}
```

Including DrawGuide(); at the end of the Update function ensures that the guide will get positioned correctly during every frame of the game. Save the GameController script and play the design game to see the guide in action.

If you play the design game for a bit you'll probably feel that, even with the guide, it's still a bit difficult to determine where the falling block will land on the stack. As a further aid, some alternate views can be provided. The player should be able to view the GameBoard from the front, top and side to more easily see where the current block will land. Write the code below in the SetView function.

Listing 2.15 The SetView function.

```
function SetView (view : int)
{
    if (view == 1)
    {
        transform.position = cam_pos_1;
        transform.LookAt(Vector3(0, 0, 0));
    } else if (view == 2) {
```

```
        transform.position = cam_pos_2;
        transform.LookAt(Vector3(0, 0, 0));
    } else if (view == 3) {
        transform.position = cam_pos_3;
        transform.LookAt(Vector3(0, 0, 0));
    }
}
```

This function requires an argument named `view` that is an integer. The value of this argument corresponds to which of the three views of the GameBoard is desired: 1 for front, 2 for top or 3 for side. There is an if statement that tests for which view is being requested. Inside each section of the if statement, the first line starts out with `transform.position`. When transform is used without any preceding reference to a game object, e.g. some_object. transform, it refers to the transform data (position, scale, rotation) of the object to which this script is attached. Since you attached this script to the Main Camera in the 'Defining Variables' section, transform refers to the placement of the camera. In each of the transform.position lines, the position of the Main Camera is set equal to one of three vectors that you previously defined: cam_pos_1, cam_pos_2 and cam_pos_3. These vectors refer to points at which the camera should be placed to view the scene from the front, top and side respectively. The second line, reading '`transform.LookAt(0, 0, 0);`', uses a function called LookAt to rotate the Main Camera so that it is pointed at the origin, which corresponds to the center of the GameBoard.

With the SetView function complete, a few more lines of code in the Update function will allow switching between the views using the keyboard.

Listing 2.16 Calling the SetView function from the Update function when keys are pressed.

```
. . .
    if (Input.GetKeyUp(KeyCode.Space))
    {
        paused = !paused;
    }
    if (Input.GetKeyUp("1"))
    {
        SetView(1);
    }
    if (Input.GetKeyUp("2"))
    {
```

```
        SetView(2);
    }
    if (Input.GetKeyUp("3"))
    {
        SetView(3);
    }
    DrawGuide();
}
```

Can you read and understand this code? Note the similarity between the existing code at the top that pauses the game and the new code. These three if statements added to the Update function test to see if the 1, 2 or 3 keys have been pressed and, if so, executes the SetView function passing along the number of the view. Save the GameController script and test out this new functionality.

Fig. 2.9 Three views, from left to right: front, top, side.

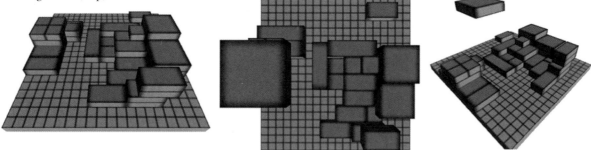

2.12 · Starting Over

'The Proposal' section discussed several ways to make this design game more engaging. One of these was to include a built-in time limit. Using the logic of Tetris, a simple method can accomplish this goal. The design game should stop if the player stacks their blocks over a certain height. When each block touches down, a test will be needed to determine whether that block has been stacked too high. If this is the case, the current stacking session will end and the player will have the opportunity to start again with a clean board. The test will happen in the Update function.

Listing 2.17 An excerpt of the Update function showing the test for ending a game.

```
...
if (HasTouchedDown())
```

```
{
     if (current_block.transform.position.y > 8)
     {
          game_over = true;
          paused = true;
          current_block.renderer.material.SetColor("_Color", Color.
red);
     } else {
          current_block.tag = "Landed";
          current_block = next_block;
          current_block.transform.position = start_point;
          next_block = CreateBlock();
     }
} else {
     current_block.transform.position.y -= falling_step;
}
...
```

The if statement introduced here tests whether the height of the current block is above eight units. If it's not, the code in the else section continues to create new blocks just as before. If the height is greater than eight, meaning this stack of blocks is now nine high, the game ends. The game_over and paused variables are set to true to prohibit further play.

The final line in this section colors the current block red to indicate that it has been stacked too high. Here SetColor is a function that is part of the material that has been applied to current_block. Recall from the Prefab section of this chapter, that materials are applied to objects to define their color, texture and other visual qualities. Here the SetColor function is used to change the color of the material applied to current_block to red.

Save the GameController script and click play. If you allow the blocks to fall without moving them, the ninth block to fall onto the stack will turn red and the game will pause.

Now that the game has an end, there needs to be a way to restart it with a clean board. You can write some code in the StartOver function that will do this. How much of it do you recall from the previous code you have written?

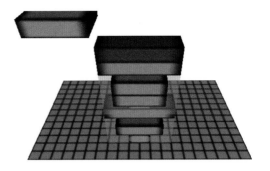

Fig. 2.10 The final block turning red.

Listing 2.18 The StartOver function.

```
function StartOver() {
    Destroy(current_block);
    Destroy(next_block);
    var landed_blocks =
        GameObject.FindGameObjectsWithTag("Landed");
    for (landed_block in landed_blocks)
    {
        Destroy(landed_block);
    }
    current_block = CreateBlock();
    current_block.transform.position = start_point;
    next_block = CreateBlock();
    next_step = Time.time + time_step;
    game_over = false;
    paused = false;
}
```

Here, a function named **Destroy** is used to delete all of the blocks in the scene. Destroy requires an argument that specifies which game object it should delete. The first two lines inside the function delete the current_block and the next_block objects. Then an array is created containing a list of all the blocks that have been tagged with "Landed". This line and the for loop that follows are just like those you wrote in the HasTouchedDown function. Each block in the array is destroyed one by one in the for loop. The four lines following the for loop are taken directly from the Start function. They create a new current_block and a new next_block and position the current_block at the start_point, ready to fall. The next_step variable is also updated with a new time.

There needs to be a way for the player to reset the design game. You've already written code that allows the space bar to pause the game. A few modifications to the Update function can have it be the trigger to restart as well.

Listing 2.19 An excerpt from the Update function showing reset code.

```
...
if (Input.GetKeyUp(KeyCode.Space))
{
    if (game_over)
    {
        StartOver();
    } else {
        paused - !paused;
    }
}
...
```

The added if statement tests for whether the game_over variable is true. If it isn't, the paused variable is set to its opposite as before. If game_over is true, then the StartOver function is called and the game restarts. Save the GameController script and try pressing the space bar once the last block turns red.

2.13 · Interface

The very last task in creating the Building Blocks design game is to write some code that will create buttons and text. This code goes in the OnGUI function in the GameController script.

Listing 2.20 The OnGUI function.

```
function OnGUI ()
{
    if (game_over)
    {
      var box_pos = Rect(((Screen.width / 2) - 150),
                          ((Screen.height / 2) - 100),
                          300, 200);
      GUI.Box(box_pos, "Game Over!");
      var button_pos = Rect(((Screen.width / 2) - 100),
                            ((Screen.height / 2) - 50),
                            200, 100);
      if (GUI.Button(button_pos, "Play Again"))
      {
          StartOver();
      }
```

```
    }
    GUI.Box(Rect(10, 10, 100, 400), "Building Blocks");
    GUILayout.BeginArea(Rect(20, 40, 80, 360));
    if (paused)
    {
        if (GUILayout.Button("Play"))
        {
            paused = false;
        }
    } else {
        if (GUILayout.Button("Pause"))
        {
            paused = true;
        }
    }
    GUILayout.Label("View:");
    if (GUILayout.Button("Front"))
    {
        SetView(1);
    }
    if (GUILayout.Button("Top"))
    {
        SetView(2);
    }
    if (GUILayout.Button("Side"))
    {
        SetView(3);
    }
    GUILayout.Label("Press arrow keys to move blocks.");
    GUILayout.Label("Press R to rotate blocks.");
    GUILayout.Label("Press space to pause.");
    GUILayout.Label("Press 1, 2 or 3 to change view.");
    if (GUILayout.Button("Restart"))
    {
        StartOver();
    }
    GUILayout.EndArea();
}
```

Find out more about graphical user interfaces in Unity under the Additional Resources section in the Chapter 2 section of the companion website.

OnGUI is a function with a specific role in Unity scripts. The code inside draws two-dimensional graphics on top of the three-dimensional scene. GUI, typically pronounced 'gooey', is an acronym that stands for graphical user interface. Almost all software has a GUI made of text, images, buttons, sliders, checkboxes, menus and other elements that allow the user to control the software. Unity has a collection of functions for creating all of these interface elements. I will briefly go over some of these functions here, but there will be more in-depth examples as the book progresses.

The first piece of the OnGUI function is an if statement that draws two items on the screen if game_over equals true. The first is a `GUI.Box` which appears as a translucent box. The `box_pos` variable on the line above refers to a `Rect`, or rectangle, object. This variable serves as the first argument for the GUI.Box function and defines the upper-left corner, width and height of the box. `Screen.width` and `Screen.height` are equal to the dimensions of the game screen in pixels. The second argument serves as the label that will show up at the top of the box, in this case the phrase "Game Over!".

The next interface element is a `GUI.Button` function with the label "Play Again", located inside the parentheses of an if statement. This brings up an interesting aspect of GUI.Button and other GUI functions. Not only do each of the GUI functions draw elements onto the screen, they also return a result if that element has been clicked or changed. This allows buttons, which return true if clicked, to trigger some action. If the button labeled "Play Again" is clicked, then the StartOver function will be executed, restarting the game.

Find the line that executes the GUI.Box function with the label "Building Blocks". The box that this line creates will appear as a rectangle on the screen and serve as a backdrop on top of which the rest of the interface elements will be placed. Including the following buttons and text inside this box will visually group them into a set of related elements.

The interface elements so far have required data about their position and size before they could be drawn. The remaining interface elements in the OnGUI function will be automatically sized and positioned using a different, but related, set of functions. These functions use the prefix `GUILayout` instead of GUI. For instance, GUI.Button and GUILayout.Button can both create a button and test if it's been clicked. The GUILayout version, however, doesn't require any positioning or size information, just a label. Often video game developers want to position interface elements very precisely using the GUI prefix. For the purposes of this and other projects in this book, GUILayout will help save time by making this process automatic.

The `GUILayout.BeginArea` function defines an invisible rectangle that will act as a container for the elements that follow. All of the elements between GUILayout.BeginArea and `GUILayout.EndArea` will be automatically positioned and sized to fill the container. If the Rect that defines this area is changed, all of the buttons and text in it will change as well.

The first element inside this container is a button that allows the player to pause and play the game. The if statement creates a button labeled "Play" if the variable paused is true and one labeled "Pause" if paused is false. If either of these buttons is clicked, paused is set equal to its opposite. In effect, this will create a single button that will allow the player to pause and play the game, the same function that the space bar serves.

The next element inside the container is a `GUILayout.Label` function that will print "Views:" to the screen. This labels the three buttons that follow, each of which is in an if statement to test for clicks. The buttons are labeled "Front", "Top" and "Side". If any are clicked the SetView function is executed to change the camera position, just as the 1, 2 and 3 keys do.

The last button is labeled "Restart". If clicked, this button will execute the StartOver function. This will allow the player to restart the game at any time, not only when blocks have been stacked too high. The final line inside the OnGUI function, GUILayout.EndArea, closes the container started with GUILayout.BeginArea. These two functions always need to be paired.

Save the GameController script one last time and play the design game to try out the new interface. Be sure to test all of the buttons to be sure they work. If you allow the blocks to stack nine high, you should see the game over message along with the button to play again.

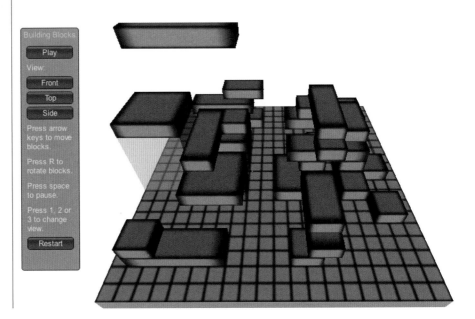

Fig. 2.11 The completed Building Blocks design game.

2.14 · Further Exploration

Congratulations on completing your first design game! You've gone through the entire process from receiving a brief from a designer to translating it into a working design game. Along the way you learned how to write code that moves objects around, responds to player input and determines how the design game progresses. Creating a simple version of Tetris might seem like a small accomplishment, but you now know many of the skills that will allow you to take on the more complex and creative projects to come.

Suppose that Pat, our designer friend from the Brief section of this chapter, has tried out your new Building Blocks design game. Inspired by your work, he now has a few ideas for how to improve it. Using your newly acquired knowledge, consider how you might meet the following challenges:

- Pat would like to see four more sizes of blocks, for a total of eight. How would you add four new size options to the randomly chosen blocks?
- Pat wants to be able to speed up or slow down the game play, depending on his mood. How would you go about increasing the speed at which the blocks fall?
- Not all the blocks that fall are desirable at the time they're created. Pat would like to be able to 'throw away' a block if he doesn't think it will be useful to him. How could you allow him to reject a block and move on to the next one?

Chapter 3

SLINGSHOT

3.1 · The Brief

Amanda works as a designer at an architecture firm. She has been working nonstop lately on plans for a housing development. Most of this work has involved drawings of wood framing details. In the United States, the structure of most houses is composed of a frame made out of lumber. These pieces are referred to by their cross-sectional dimensions in inches – two by fours, two by sixes, two by twelves, etc. Amanda has been drawing assemblies of these elements over and over again for weeks and needs a break. She wants a game that would allow her to vent her frustration about this work in brief sessions throughout the day. Her idea is a design game in which she would get to throw these pieces of lumber around to express her frustration. She thinks this type of design game could help blow off steam and provide a new venue for some creative expression. Amanda feels like it may help her to assemble these standard components into novel forms that could reveal new creative possibilities.

3.2 · The Proposal

This design game will be titled Slingshot. Play will involve throwing lumber that sticks together to form assemblages like the one in Figure 3.1. In order to achieve the intensity and quickness that Amanda asked for in the brief, you'll add several elements that will constrain the play in productive ways. The first addition will be a playing field – essentially a box with one open side. This will give the player a target to aim at as well as surfaces off of which they can bounce the lumber that they launch. The bouncing behavior will make bank shots possible, as in pool or basketball, giving the player the option of sticking new pieces onto the sides or back of the lumber assemblage.

In the previous chapter you created a variety of differently sized blocks by making copies of a simple prefab. For Slingshot, you will be able to use the same method to create various sizes of lumber. In order to allow Amanda to 'throw' the lumber and have it bounce off walls, it will be necessary to learn about physics simulation. Using physics, you'll be able to create objects that can be thrown through the air and collide with other objects in a realistic way. You'll create a simple mechanism for loading, aiming and launching the lumber at the walls that behaves like a slingshot. This will give the interaction in Slingshot both speed and the kind of visceral quality that Amanda seems to be after.

Fig. 3.1 Example Assemblage.

Like the Building Blocks project, this design game will employ some ran-domness to make the assemblages unpredictable. When each piece of lumber is loaded, its size will be randomly chosen from among five standard sizes. You'll also add a time limit and scoring that will reward quick and spontane-ous play.

3.3 · Opening the Project

To get started, open the SlingshotStarter project which you can find in the Slingshot folder inside the DesignGamesResources package you downloaded. Refer to the first chapter of this book 'Tools of the Trade' for instructions on how this is done. Once the project is open, double-click MainScene in the Project pane to ensure that the scene you will be working in is active.

In the Scene pane as well as the Hierarchy pane you'll see four objects. There is a camera, which all scenes require, called MainCamera. In addition to providing a view of the scene, the camera also has a script attached named GameController. You will add code to this script that will control how this design game works. There are two lights in the scene that will provide illumination. Finally there is an object named PlayBox. By clicking the tri-angle next to its name, you can see that the PlayBox is actually composed of six boxes with names like FaceBack, FaceBottom, etc. When the player 'slingshots' pieces of lumber into the scene, these boxes will contain them inside the playing area. The player will also be able to use them to make bank shots, bouncing the lumber off of the sides of the PlayBox.

Take a look at the various items in the Project pane. There are prefabs, materials, textures and scripts provided for you here. You'll learn the purpose of each of these as you build the Slingshot project.

3.4 · Ready

The very first step in building this design game is to create a mechanism whereby the player can load pieces of lumber in various sizes. There will need to be some kind of graphical interface on the screen that the player can click to accomplish this. You'll create a bullseye in the center of the screen that will serve this purpose. Looking in the Project pane, open GameController in the scripts folder by double-clicking on it. You should see the script editor open up and load the GameController script.

Listing 3.1 The DrawSight function (existing code in gray).

```
function DrawSight ()
{
    if ( !cameraIsRotating && !displayGameOver )
    {
        if ( sightIsEngaged )
        {
            if ( Input.GetMouseButtonUp(0) )
            {
                sightIsEngaged = false;
                LaunchCurrentLumber();
            }
        } else {
            if ( sightRect.Contains(Input.mousePosition) )
            {
                GUI.DrawTexture(    sightRect,
                                    sightTextureActive,
                                ScaleMode.ScaleToFit,
                                    true, 1.0 );
                if ( Input.GetMouseButtonDown(0) )
                {
                    sightIsEngaged = true;
                    currentLumber = CreateLumber();
```

```
            }
        } else {
            GUI.DrawTexture(    sightRect, sightTexture,
                                ScaleMode.ScaleToFit,
                                true, 1.0 );
        }
    }
}
```

When you first take a look at the GameController script, you'll see that a bunch of code has been provided. Mostly this code consists of variable definitions and empty functions that you'll use as you build up the functionality of this design game.

Locate the DrawSight function and type in the code as you see it in Listing 3.1. This is the code that will draw the sight, a bullseye icon, to the screen. Inside the function there is an if statement that checks the value of two variables: `cameraIsRotating` and `displayGameOver`. You will write the new code inside the braces of this if statement. Its purpose will become clear later.

The new code also makes use of an if statement. Inside the parentheses is a single condition: the variable `sightIsEngaged`. It is a boolean variable that can have the value true or false. The first block of code inside the first set of braces will happen if this variable is true and the block after the `else` will happen if it is false. In this way the sightIsEngaged variable will act as a switch from one set of functionality and another. To start off, sightIsEngaged will be false and a gray bullseye will be drawn in the center of the screen. When the player clicks on the bullseye, it will change color to indicate that it is engaged. Then when the player releases the mouse, the bullseye will return to its original state. This will provide the slingshot behavior by which the player loads, aims and fires the lumber at the PlayBox.

Take a look at the line immediately following the `}` `else` `{` line. This if statement has the condition `sightRect.Contains(Input.mousePosition)`. The sightRect variable is a Rect, a type of object that defines a two-dimensional rectangle on the screen. It's used here to lay out where on the screen the bullseye icon should go. Rect objects have a function named 'Contains' that can determine whether or not a given point is within their boundaries or not. The dot in `sightRect.Contains` means that the Contains function is a part of the sightRect object. Objects like Rects are abstract, imaginary objects that don't have any visible presence but offer useful functionality.

Here the Contains function will be true if the mouse cursor is over the bullseye sight.

If the mouse cursor is inside the sightRect, the `GUI.DrawTexture` function puts a dark colored bullseye in the center of the screen. The DrawTexture function takes five arguments which are inside the parentheses and separated by commas. In this case these arguments are `sightRect`, `sightTextureAc-`, `tive`, `ScaleMode.ScaleToFit`, `true`, `1.0`. The last three of these arguments determine some aspects of how the texture – an image – appears. These will typically be the same values for most textures. You can read more about these settings in the Unity scripting reference online. The first two arguments, sightRect and sightTextureActive, are the important ones to understand. As explained above, the sightRect defines where on the screen the texture will appear. The actual image that will be placed on the screen is specified by sightTextureActive. If you return to the main Unity window and highlight the MainCamera, you can see 'Sight Texture Active' in the list of variables in the Inspector pane. To the right of the name should be 'SightActive', the name of an image in the Textures folder visible in the Project pane. If you wanted to have a different image appear in place of the SightActive texture, you could drag that new image from the Project pane onto 'Sight Texture Active' in the Inspector.

Find the line that reads `if ( Input.GetMouseButtonDown(0) )`. This if statement tests for whether the player has clicked the mouse button while the cursor was over the bullseye icon. If this happens the sightIsEngaged variable is set to true and a variable named currentLumber is set to the results of a function named CreateLumber. You'll explore the CreateLumber function in a bit, but as its name suggests, this is how a new piece of lumber will be made.

The if statement with the condition `sightRect.Contains( Input.mouse-Position )` has an else block toward the end of the DrawSight function. Inside the braces of this block is another `GUI.DrawTexture` function. This code is exactly like the previous DrawTexture code, except the texture to draw is sightTexture, a lighter bullseye image. This code will execute when the sightIsEngaged variable is false and the mouse cursor is not over the bullseye icon. So if the player isn't interacting at all, a light gray bullseye will be displayed. If they move the mouse over the icon, a darker gray icon will be displayed to indicate that they can click on it to load a new piece of lumber.

If you try the game out now, you can see that clicking on the bullseye sight creates a box. This is a copy of a prefab called Lumber located in

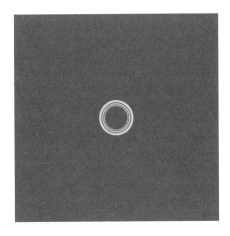 

Fig. 3.2 Light gray sight displayed by default and the darker sight displayed when the mouse cursor is on top of it.

the Project pane. It is made in the CreateLumber function that appears in the DrawSight function. When you add the following code to that function, these copies will get created in various sizes corresponding to standard lumber used in the United States.

Listing 3.2 The CreateLumber function.

```
function CreateLumber () : GameObject
{
    var new_lumber = Instantiate( lumberPrefab,
                                  lumberStartPosition,
                                  Quaternion.identity );
    var lumber_scale;
    var r = Random.value;
    if ( r < 0.2 )
    {
        lumber_scale = Vector3( 0.2, 0.2, 8.0 );
    } else if ( r >= 0.2 && r < 0.4 ) {
        lumber_scale = Vector3( 0.4, 0.2, 8.0 );
    } else if ( r >= 0.4 && r < 0.6 ) {
        lumber_scale = Vector3( 0.4, 0.4, 8.0 );
    } else if ( r >= 0.6 && r < 0.8 ) {
        lumber_scale = Vector3( 0.2, 0.6, 8.0 );
    } else {
        lumber_scale = Vector3( 1.2, 0.2, 8.0 );
    }
    new_lumber.transform.localScale = lumber_scale;
    return new_lumber;
}
```

65

If you think back to the Building Blocks project in Chapter 2, this code should look a bit familiar. The existing lines create a new copy of the Lumber prefab and return it. While functions aren't required to have a final line with the keyword 'return', many times it is useful to have a function answer back, or return, a value. When this is the case, the function needs to specify what type of data it is sending back. Here this is accomplished on the very first line: `function CreateLumber () : GameObject`. Any data that goes into the function goes inside the parentheses and the type of data that comes out is specified after a colon. The colon can be read as 'returns data of type'. This function returns a GameObject; a new copy of the Lumber prefab.

The complicated looking code that you added to this function is very similar to the code you used to create blocks of various sizes in the Building Blocks project. A variable named 'r' is set to a random value. The if statement that follows sets the value of lumber_scale to different values based on where the 'r' variable falls between zero and one. The lumber_scale variable is a Vector3 object that will define the width, height and depth of the new copy of the Lumber prefab. This scale gets set in the line `new_lumber.transform.localScale = lumberScale`. So there is a 20 percent chance that new_lumber will be any of the five different sizes specified in the if statement. If you save this script and try out the design game now, you should see new pieces of lumber in different sizes appear in the center of the screen when you click on the sight.

3.5 · Aim

Lumber in several standard sizes can now be created. Next, you need to provide a way for the player to aim these pieces at different targets within the PlayBox. You can accomplish this by tracking where the player moves the mouse after clicking on the sight to load a piece of lumber. This is where the slingshot style interaction comes in. The player will click on the sight to load some lumber, pull back to aim and then release to launch. The aiming portion of this happens with a few lines of code in the Update function.

Listing 3.3 Aiming code in the Update function.

```
function Update ()
{
    RecordMouse();
    RotateCamera();
```

```
    if ( sightIsEngaged )
    {
        currentLumber.transform.position =
        Vector3( mousePosition.x * aimingRatio,
    mousePosition.y * aimingRatio,
    lumberStartPosition.z );
    }
}
```

Inside the Update function, you are adding an if statement that checks whether the isSightEngaged variable is true. This means that the player has clicked on the sight and is now aiming the lumber. Within the if statement the position of currentLumber, `currentLumber.transform.position`, is set to a new Vector3 that refers to a point in space. When a new copy of the Lumber prefab is produced in the CreateLumber function, it is positioned at a point called lumberStartPosition. In the DrawSight function, this new lumber object is stored in a variable named currentLumber. This variable will always refer to the piece of lumber that the player is currently aiming. The x and y location of currentLumber are set here using a variable named mousePosition. You'll see how this variable is created next. The aimingRatio that gets multiplied with the mousePosition numbers (e.g. mousePosition.x * aimingRatio) is a number that ensures that the currentLumber object is directly under the mouse cursor when the player is aiming. You can alter the values of aimingRatio and lumberStartPosition in the Inspector when you have the MainCamera highlighted in the Hierarchy. I've set them to good values for you already, but you can change them to see what effect they have.

Listing 3.4 The RecordMouse function.

```
function RecordMouse ()
{
    mousePrevious.x = mousePosition.x;
    mousePrevious.y = mousePosition.y;
    mousePosition.x = Input.mousePosition.x - screenOrigin.x;
    mousePosition.y = Input.mousePosition.y - screenOrigin.y;
    mouseDelta.x = (mousePosition.x - mousePrevious.x) /
                   (Screen.width / 2);
    mouseDelta.y = (mousePosition.y - mousePrevious.y) /
                   (Screen.height / 2);
}
```

RecordMouse is a function that updates three variables: mousePrevious, mousePosition and mouseDelta. To get the location of the mouse cursor on the screen, you would use `Input.mousePosition`, which contains the current x and y coordinates. These coordinates are measured from the top, left corner of the screen with the positive x axis extending to the right and the positive y axis extending down. The three-dimensional space of this scene, however, has its origin at the center of the screen. If you used Input.mousePosition to set the location of the currentLumber object, it wouldn't show up under the mouse cursor. You can test this by adding `Input.` in front of `mousePosition.x` and `mousePosition.y` in the Update function. This behavior is corrected in the `mousePosition.x` and `mousePosition.y` lines in the RecordMouse function. The screenOrigin variable used here is set to the x and y coordinates of the center of the screen. If your design game was displayed in a window 800 pixels across and 600 pixels down, then screenOrigin.x would be 400 and screenOrigin.y would be 300. When subtracted from the corresponding mouse coordinates, this gives mousePosition values that match up with the three-dimensional scene. Save the GameController script and test out the design game. You should be able to click on the sight and have the resulting lumber object follow your mouse around the screen.

3.6 · Fire

Now that the player can load and aim pieces of lumber, it's time to get them to launch. You can use Unity's physics simulation capabilities to accomplish this. There are two components that need to be added to an object to enable physics. The first is called a collider. With a collider, objects can detect when they come in contact with other objects. It also determines how objects hit each other and how they bounce off each other. When a primitive shape like the Lumber prefab is created it has a collider attached to it by default. By itself this handles collision detection, but to enable the Lumber prefab to bounce off other surfaces, you'll need to add something called a physics material. These are special materials that specify how an object physically behaves. Aspects like friction, bounciness and others can be set using physics materials. Be sure the Lumber prefab is selected in the Project pane, then add the included LumberPhysics material by dragging it onto the collider component.

Learn more about how colliders work in the Chapter 3 section of the companion website.

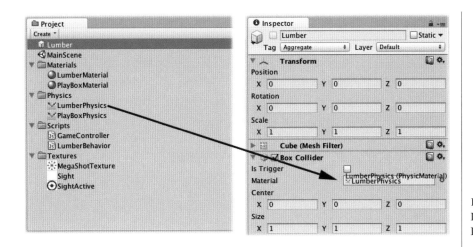

Fig. 3.3 Adding the LumberPhysics material to the Lumber prefab.

The next step is to add the rigid body component that will handle the simulation of physical motion. With the Lumber prefab still selected, select **Component > Physics > Rigidbody** from the main menu.

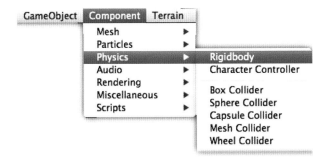

Fig. 3.4 Adding a rigid body component to the Lumber prefab.

A rigid body component has a few parameters that define its behavior. Set these parameters as shown below.

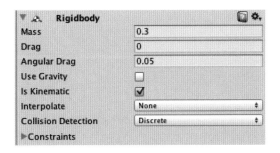

Fig. 3.5 Rigidbody configuration.

All of the settings for the rigid body can be left at their default values except for three. Set the mass to 0.3 which will speed up the speed at which the lumber moves. Uncheck the 'Use Gravity' setting so the lumber won't fall down as it travels. Finally uncheck the 'Is Kinematic' setting to ensure that the lumber doesn't move until it is launched. If a rigid body is kinematic, it means that the object it's attached to won't move automatically.

With the rigid body configured, you can now write a bit of code to launch the lumber when the player releases the mouse button.

Listing 3.5 The LaunchCurrentLumber function.

```
function LaunchCurrentLumber ()
{
    currentLumber.rigidbody.isKinematic = false;
    var launch_vector = launchThroughPoint -
    currentLumber.transform.position;
    var launch_force =  launch_vector * ( Random.Range(50, 200)
                        * forceMultiplier );
    currentLumber.rigidbody.AddForce(launch_force);
    var launch_torque = Vector3.right * ( Random.Range(-200,
            200) * torqueMultiplier );
    currentLumber.rigidbody.AddTorque(launch_torque);
}
```

In the first line of the LaunchCurrentLumber function, the isKinematic property is set to false to enable the currentLumber object to move on its own. Next a vector variable named launch_vector is created. This happens by subtracting the position of currentLumber from launchThroughPoint, a point in between the camera and the origin. Since the currentLumber object is positioned where the mouse cursor is, this results in a vector that points from the currentLumber object through the launchThroughPoint.

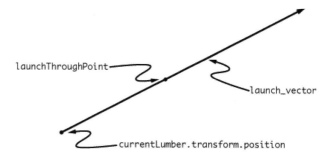

launchThroughPoint

launch_vector

currentLumber.transform.position

Fig. 3.6 Calculating launch_vector.

The second line in the LaunchCurrentLumber function takes launch_vector and multiplies it by a random number and then by a number variable named forceMultiplier. The result is a scaled version of launch_vector which is stored in the launch_force variable. Next this vector is used to add some speed and trajectory to currentLumber via the AddForce function. If you imagine a vector as a rubber band stretched from one point to another, the AddForce function is like releasing the energy stored in it.

Listing 3.6 Calling the LaunchCurrentLumber function from the DrawSight function.

```
if ( sightIsEngaged )
{
    if ( Input.GetMouseButtonUp(0) )
    {
        sightIsEngaged = false;
        LaunchCurrentLumber();
    }
} else {
```

For a refresher on vector mathematics, see Additional Resources in the Chapter 3 section of the companion website.

By adding the new line of code above to the DrawSight function, you can complete the launching functionality. Recall that the DrawSight function changes the sight texture in the middle of the screen when the player clicks on it. The sight remains a darker color as the player drags the mouse, then switches back to the default when the mouse button is released. Now when this happens the currentLumber object will launch toward the PlayBox. Save the script and try launching a few yourself.

3.7 · Aggregation

Lumber is getting created and launched, but it's not yet aggregating together like the brief outlined. To accomplish this, you'll need to add some code to the LumberBehavior script. Since this script is attached to the Lumber prefab, any code you add will define the functionality of every piece of lumber created. You can find the file under the scripts folder in the Project pane. Open it up by double-clicking on it. At the top of the script you'll see that there are three variables defined. You'll see how these work as you flesh out the lumberBehavior script.

Listing 3.7 The Start function in the LumberBehavior script.

```
function Start ()
{
    var box_top = GameObject.Find("FaceTop");
```

```
        var box_width = box_top.transform.localScale.x - 2.0;
    playBounds = Bounds( Vector3.zero, Vector3(box_width,
            box_width, box_width) );
    mainCamera = GameObject.Find("MainCamera");
    rigidbody.detectCollisions = false;
}
```

Code inside the Start function gets executed immediately after the object which it's attached to is created. Since the LumberBehavior script is attached to the Lumber prefab, these instructions will be carried out for each piece of lumber made. The first three lines serve to construct the playBounds variable. Look at the line starting 'playBounds'. A Bounds object is like an imaginary box with a center and size. This one will record the boundary of the PlayBox. It is created using two vectors which are `Vector3.zero`, corresponding to the center point (the origin) and `Vector3(box_width, box_width, box_width)` which defines the width, height and depth. In the preceding line, box_width is defined as the x dimension of the box_top object, minus a margin of two. Recall that a transform stores the position, rotation and size of an object. The localScale property of a transform contains the x, y and z dimensions. The box_top variable refers to the FaceTop object, which is the top face of the PlayBox. Accounting for the two units subtracted from box_width, playBounds corresponds to the interior dimensions of the PlayBox.

The mainCamera variable is set equal to the MainCamera. This is necessary so that this script can send messages to the GameController script that is attached to the MainCamera. In the final line of the Start function, `rigidbody.detectCollisions` is set to false. The rigidBody component is what allows the lumber object to react in a physical manner. By setting detectCollisions to false, you're making sure that each piece of lumber will ignore its collision with the PlayBox when it's launched. This ensures that the pieces will fly through the invisible front face of the PlayBox. Further along in this script you'll turn this back on so the lumber can bounce off of the interior.

Listing 3.8 The Update function in the LumberBehavior script.

```
function Update ()
{
    if ( !rigidbody.detectCollisions &&
        playBounds.Contains(transform.position) )
    {
```

```
        rigidbody.detectCollisions = true;
    }
}
```

Inside the Update function goes the switch to turn on collision detection. The if statement's two conditions are separated by a && symbol, meaning they both must be true for the code inside the braces to execute. The first, `!rigidbody.detectCollisions`, indicates that collision detection should still be turned off. The second, `playBounds.Contains(transform.position)`, specifies that this lumber object should be inside the PlayBox. Contains is a function of any Bounds object that can take a point, in this case the current position of this lumber object, and determine whether it is inside its extents. If these conditions are both true, then detectCollisions is set to true for this object and it can sense when it runs into the interior of the PlayBox or any of the other lumber objects.

Listing 3.9 The OnCollisionEnter function in the LumberBehavior script.

```
function OnCollisionEnter ( collision : Collision )
{
    if ( collision.gameObject.tag == "Stuck" )
    {
        gameObject.tag = "Stuck";
        rigidbody.detectCollisions = false;
        rigidbody.isKinematic = true;
        mainCamera.SendMessage("IncrementAssemblageCount");
    }
}
```

The OnCollisionEnter function is a built-in function in Unity like Start, Update and others. It gets called whenever an object, like the lumber objects to which this script is attached, come in contact with another object. The collision argument that it takes refers to the object that was hit. An if statement checks whether the colliding object has the tag "Stuck". If this is the case, it can stop 'thinking' about what it needs to do. The only lumber objects with the tag "Stuck" are those already in the center assemblage. Once this piece runs into any of the pieces in the assemblage, it has fulfilled its duty.

To stick the piece of lumber in its place, its tag is switched to "Stuck", ensuring that other pieces that come along will also stick to this object. Next, detectCollisions is set to false so that this object doesn't keep checking the same collision it just had over and over. The isKinematic parameter is set to true so that physics simulation doesn't continue. Finally, a message is sent to the MainCamera using the SendMessage function. This calls a function – in this case IncrementAssemblageCount – in any script attached to the specified object – here the MainCamera object. The IncrementAssemblageCount function, in the GameController script, will be called and increase the score by one.

3.8 · Getting a Better View

Now that your design game can create big masses of lumber, you need to provide a way for the player to take a better look at what they have created. The following code does just that. It should all go inside the RotateCamera function. If you look in the Update function, you'll see that RotateCamera gets called every frame.

What went wrong? Test out the design game at this point. If there are any problems, look at the Chapter 3 section of the companion website for tips.

Listing 3.10 The RotateCamera function.

```
function RotateCamera ()
{
    if ( Input.GetMouseButtonDown(0) &&
        !sightRect.Contains(Input.mousePosition) )
    {
        cameraIsRotating = true;
    }
    if ( cameraIsRotating )
    {
        if ( Input.GetMouseButton(0) )
        {
            cameraRotation.x -= mouseDelta.y;
            cameraRotation.y += mouseDelta.x;
            transform.position = cameraRotation *
cameraDefaultPosition;
            transform.LookAt( Vector3.zero );
        }
        if ( Input.GetMouseButtonUp(0) )
        {
            cameraIsRotating = false;
            cameraRotation = Quaternion.identity;
        }
    } else {
        if ( transform.position != cameraDefaultPosition )
        {
```

```
                    transform.position = Vector3.MoveTowards(
                                        transform.position,
                                        cameraDefaultPosition,
                                        cameraSpeed );
                    transform.LookAt( Vector3.zero );
            }
        }
    }
```

The complicated looking code inside this RotateCamera function really just does three things. It checks for whether the player has pressed the mouse button, moves the camera if they drag the mouse and returns the camera to its original position if they release the button. All of this is made possible by the two if statements inside the function.

Starting at the top, an if statement tests for whether two conditions, separated by the symbol && (meaning 'and'), are both true. The first of these conditions, Input.GetMouseButtonDown(0), is true if the player has just pressed the primary (usually left) mouse button down during this frame. The second condition, !sightRect.Contains(Input.mousePosition), is true if the mouse cursor is not inside the aiming sight. This area is defined by a Rect object called sightRect. All Rect objects have a function called Contains which returns true or false depending on whether the point given as the argument is inside (true) or outside (false) its boundary. Prior to this condition there is a ! symbol, which turns whatever follows into its opposite. Consequently this condition actually tests if the mouse is not over the area of the sight. If the player presses the mouse button and the mouse cursor is not over the sight, then the variable cameraIsRotating is set to true.

After this first if statement is another one that checks whether cameraIsRotating is true. If it is, two more if statements are evaluated. One with Input.GetMouseButton(0) runs some code if the mouse button is still being held down. Inside are some instructions for moving the position of the camera according to how the mouse is moving. A variable called cameraRotation gets modified with the mouseDelta values that are recorded each frame in the RecordMouse function discussed earlier. Why does mouseDelta.y get subtracted from cameraRotation.x and mouseDelta.x get added to cameraRotation.y? The easiest way to find this out is to see it in action. Try saving the script and running the design game with this new code. You should be able to click and drag the mouse anywhere outside the sight to rotate the camera. Now stop the game and change those two cameraRotation lines to `cameraRotation.x += mouseDelta.x;` and `cameraRotation.y += mouseDelta.y;` respectively. If you run the game and try dragging the mouse now, you should notice a big difference in the movement. Dragging the mouse up and down moves the scene left and right. Dragging left or right rotates the scene up or down. This behavior is due to the fact that rotations in Unity are specified in degrees around an axis. Since the x axis extends horizontally across the screen, cameraRotation.x specifies how much to rotate around this axis – or how much up or down. Similarly, the cameraRotation.y amount determines rotation left or right, since the y axis runs vertically. While this type of rotation certainly works, the original code provides for a more conventional experience when rotating the scene.

Under the two cameraRotation lines, the location of the camera (`transform.position`) is set to `cameraRotation * cameraDefaultPosition`. If you look back at the top of the GameController script where the variables are defined, you'll see that cameraRotation is a Quaternion and cameraDefaultPosition is a Vector3. One of the benefits of using quaternions to encode rotation is that when they are multiplied by a vector position, the result is that same position, but rotated around the origin. Since the orientation of the camera is still the same as it was initially, the last line uses the LookAt function to point the camera back at the lumber assemblage at the origin, no matter where it's located.

Locate the if statement in the code above that has the condition `Input.GetMouseButtonUp(0)`. The GetMouseButtonUp function returns true if the player has released the mouse button during the current frame. Code inside this if statement then returns the camera to its default location. The key to this movement lies in the Vector3.MoveTowards function toward the bottom of the code listing above. This function takes three arguments: a current location, a position to move towards and a speed. Respectively the arguments here are the current location of the camera (transform.position), the original location (cameraDefaultPosition) and cameraSpeed, a number that determines how fast the camera returns to its home. After the MoveTowards line is a LookAt function that keeps the camera pointed at the origin as it rotates back to its resting place. Try running the design game a few times, each time changing the cameraSpeed variable in the Inspector, with the MainCamera selected. By changing this variable, you can slow down or speed up the rate at which the camera springs back to the default position.

There is one last piece of functionality left to give the player a good view of their lumber assemblage. When the camera is rotated now, the PlayBox obscures the assemblage. An easy solution is to hide the PlayBox while the player is looking around and show it again once the camera is back at its default location. You can add this functionality with the following code.

Listing 3.11 The ShowPlayBox function.

```
function ShowPlayBox ( show : boolean )
{
    GameObject.Find("FaceBack").renderer.enabled = show;
    GameObject.Find("FaceBottom").renderer.enabled = show;
    GameObject.Find("FaceLeft").renderer.enabled = show;
    GameObject.Find("FaceRight").renderer.enabled = show;
    GameObject.Find("FaceTop").renderer.enabled = show;
}
```

The `GameObject.Find` function, as its name implies, searches for objects in the scene by name. Here you're using it to find the five sides of the PlayBox. Any object in a scene that is visible has a component called a renderer that determines its appearance. Setting the enabled parameter of a renderer to false makes the object it's attached to invisible. You can pass true or false to this ShowPlayBox function to make the sides of the PlayBox visible or invisible.

Listing 3.12 Hiding and showing the PlayBox in the RotateCamera function.

```
if ( Input.GetMouseButtonDown(0) &&
    !sightRect.Contains(Input.mousePosition) )
    {
        cameraIsRotating = true;
        ShowPlayBox(false);
    }

...

        if ( Input.GetMouseButtonUp(0) )
        {
            cameraIsRotating = false;
            cameraRotation = Quaternion.identity;
            ShowPlayBox(true);
        }
```

With the two new lines above, you are hiding the PlayBox (`ShowPlayBox(false);`) when the player starts rotating the camera and shows it (`ShowPlayBox(true);`) when the mouse button is released. If you try this

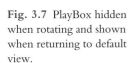

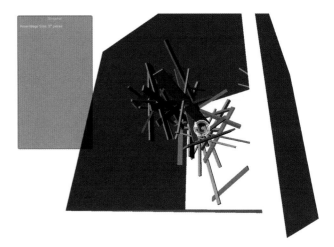

Fig. 3.7 PlayBox hidden when rotating and shown when returning to default view.

out you should be able to spin the assemblage around and have a clear view of it.

3.9 · About Time

This design game is still in need of a timer. I mentioned in the Proposal section that a time limit would help encourage the quick, spontaneous type of play that was described in the Brief. You can keep track of time in Unity quite easily, as shown in the code below.

Listing 3.13 New timer code in the Update function (existing code in gray).

```
function Update ()
{
    gameTimer -= Time.deltaTime;
    if ( gameTimer < 0.0 )
    {
        gameTimer = 0.0;
        displayGameOver = true;
    }
    RecordMouse();
    RotateCamera();
```

The first new line of code subtracts some time from a variable called gameTimer. This variable is a number that can be set in the Inspector when the MainCamera is selected in the Hierarchy. Right now it's set to 120. In Unity, time is measured in seconds, which means that at the beginning of a game, gameTimer represents two minutes (120 / 60). The Time.deltaTime value that is subtracted is equal to the amount of time that has passed during this frame. Recall that frames are rendered 30 or more times per second when a game is running. This means that the first line is subtracting about one thirtieth of a second or less each go around.

In the if statement that follows, your new code is testing for whether the value of gameTimer has fallen below zero. If it has, gameTimer is set to zero so that it doesn't start counting into negative numbers. This variable reaching zero signals the end of the game, so the displayGameOver variable is set to true. You'll refer to this variable once you add some more code to the OnGUI function.

Listing 3.14 New code to display time in the OnGUI function (existing code in gray).

```
GUILayout.BeginArea( Rect(
                    (menu_margin * 2), (menu_margin * 4),
              menu_width - (menu_margin * 2),
        menu_height - (menu_margin * 4)) );
GUILayout.Label(    "Time Remaining: " +
                    GetMinutesSeconds( gameTimer ) );
GUILayout.Label("Assemblage Size: " + lumberCount +
                " pieces");
```

The code in the last line displays the time remaining with a label that reads something like, 'Time remaining: 1:29'. The GetMinutesSeconds function takes the gameTimer variable, which represents the number of seconds left in the game, and constructs a more readable time format. I won't go into the details of this function, but you can take a look at the bottom of the GameController script to see how it works.

Listing 3.15 Code to display the game over message in the OnGUI function (existing code in gray).

```
GUILayout.EndArea();
if ( displayGameOver )
{
    var message_pos = Rect(    (Screen.width / 2) - 100,
                               (Screen.height / 2) - 100,
                               200, 200 );
    GUI.Box(message_pos, "Game Over!");
    var message_label_pos = Rect( (Screen.width / 2) - 50,
```

```
                                       (Screen.height / 2) - 50,
                                       100, 100 );
              GUI.Label( message_label_pos, "You created a " +
                     lumberCount + " piece assemblage!" );
              var button_pos = Rect(   (Screen.width / 2) - 50,
                                       (Screen.height / 2) + 20,
                                       100, 50 );
              if ( GUI.Button( button_pos, "Play Again!" ) )
              {
                     StartOver();
              }
       }
}
```

Using the code at the beginning of this section, you switched the value of displayGameOver to true when gameTimer reached zero. Because this is true, the code inside the if statement above will execute. This code creates three elements on the screen: a box, a label with a message and a button that lets the player start the game again. Before each of the functions that create these elements (`GUI.Box`, `GUI.Label` and `GUI.Button`), the result of the Rect function is stored in a variable. The Rect function takes four arguments: position along the x axis, position along the y axis, width and height. Each of the Box, Label and Button functions takes these rectangles as their first argument, setting up their position and size on the screen. Save the script and press play. If you play until the clock runs out you'll see this game over message appear in the middle of the screen. Pressing the 'Play Again!' button will call the StartOver function and reset the game.

3.10 · A Surprise

Slingshot, even in this simple form, can certainly be called a game. The player receives points for performing the required actions. Additionally, the play is constrained by a time limit, a limited range of game pieces and a finite zone of activity. Most video games also add some surprises, or bonuses, on top of these basic mechanics. Bonuses aren't an advertised part of the game, but they help encourage players as they reach goals and become more proficient. You can add a simple bonus mechanism to Slingshot with just a few lines of code. We'll call it a 'mega shot'. It will allow players to launch a bunch of lumber at once, but only after they have built up their assemblage with enough pieces.

Listing 3.16 Updated IncrementAssemblageCount function and the new AddAssemblageBonus function (existing code in gray).

```
function IncrementAssemblageCount ()
{
    lumberCount++;
    if ( lumberCount == 10 ||
         lumberCount == 20 ||
         lumberCount == 35 ||
         lumberCount % 50 == 0 )
    {
        AddAssemblageBonus();
    }
}

function AddAssemblageBonus ()
{
    timeToHideMessage = Time.time + 1.0;
    bonusMessage = "You've made a " +
    lumberCount +
    " piece assemblage! You've received a mega shot!";
    megaShotCount++;
    displayMessage = true;
}
```

In the GameController script, add the code as shown in the listing above. The if statement in the IncrementAssemblageCount function calls the new AddAssemblageBonus function if any of four conditions are met. Inside the parentheses, these conditions are separated by a double pipe symbol (||) which can be read as the word 'or'. This means that if the total number of pieces in the assemblage (stored in the lumberCount variable) is 10, 20 or 35, the new function will get called. The final condition in this set of four is a bit different. Used like this, the percent sign acts as an operator called modulo. It divides the number to its left by the one on its right and returns the remainder. So the condition 'lumberCount % 50 == 0' can be read as 'if lumberCount is evenly divisible by 50'. A bonus will be given to the player when they've reached a score of 10, 20, 35, 50 and for every 50 points they get thereafter.

Inside the AddAssemblageBonus function that you've just added is the code to give the player the bonus. Here there are four variables that get set. Time.time + 1.0 refers to a time one second in the future, which is stored in timeToHideMessage. The bonusMessage gets a string that includes the current score. One mega shot is added to `megaShotCount`. Finally, `displayMessage` is set to true. You'll see how all of these variables get used when you add the following code to the OnGUI function.

Listing 3.17 Mega shot code in the OnGUI function.

```
GUILayout.Label("Time Remaining: " +
                minutes_text + ":" + seconds_text);
GUILayout.Label("Assemblage Size: " +
                lumberCount + " pieces");
GUILayout.Label("Mega Shots: " +
                megaShotCount + " (Click to launch.)");
GUILayout.BeginHorizontal();
for ( var i = 0; i < megaShotCount; i++ )
{
    if ( GUILayout.Button( megaShotTexture,
        GUILayout.Width(36) ) )
    {
        LaunchMegaShot();
    }
}
GUILayout.EndHorizontal();
GUILayout.BeginHorizontal();
GUILayout.Label("Force: ");
```

Here you are letting the player know how many mega shots they have acquired using the first label. Next, a horizontal band establishes a place for some buttons that let the player launch the mega shots. A for loop counts up to megaShotCount and draws a button. Unlike the buttons you've seen so far, these buttons contain a texture image instead of text. In the code 'GUILayout. Button(megaShotTexture, GUILayout.Width(36))', megaShotTexture refers to the image and `GUILayout.Width` sets the width of each button to 36 pixels. To set this texture, return to the Unity editor window and select MainCamera in the Hierarchy. Drag the MegaShotTexture image from the Project pane onto 'Mega Shot Texture' in the Inspector. Finally, inside the braces of the if statement you'll see that if any of these buttons is clicked, a function called LaunchMegaShot is called.

Listing 3.18 The LaunchMegaShot function.

```
function LaunchMegaShot ()
{
    megaShotCount--;
```

```
for ( var i = 0; i < 5; i++ )
{
    currentLumber = CreateLumber();
    currentLumber.transform.position =
        Vector3( Random.Range(-3, 3),
                 Random.Range(-3, 3),
                 currentLumber.transform.position.z );
    LaunchCurrentLumber();
}
}
```

You can enter this new function anywhere in the GameController script that is outside the existing functions. In it, one is subtracted from megaShot-Count since the player has chosen to use one of their bonuses. Then a for loop counts to five. Each pass through this loop creates a new piece of lumber with the CreateLumber function, randomly positions it within a range then fires it with the LaunchCurrentLumber function. By changing the 5 in 'i < 5' you can increase or decrease the number of times this happens. Save the script and your project and try out this new function. Try increasing the number 5 to 20 in the code above to see the effect when you click on a mega shot button.

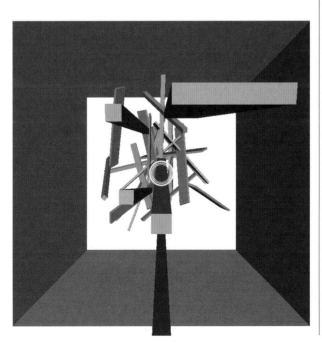

Fig. 3.8 A mega shot getting launched.

Listing 3.19 Code to show a bonus message in the OnGUI function (existing code in gray).

```
if ( GUILayout.Button("Restart") )
{
    StartOver();
}
GUILayout.EndArea();
if ( displayMessage )
{
    if ( Time.time < timeToHideMessage )
    {
        var bonus_pos = Rect(
                    (Screen.width / 2) - 100,
                    (Screen.height / 2) - 100,
                    200, 200 );
        GUI.Box( bonus_pos, "Bonus!" );
        var bonus_label_pos = Rect(
                    (Screen.width / 2) - 50,
                    (Screen.height / 2) - 50,
                    100, 100 );
        GUI.Label( bonus_label_pos, bonusMessage );
    } else {
        displayMessage = false;
    }
}
if ( displayGameOver )
{
```

The last step is to add the code above to the OnGUI function. As with the game over message you previously created, this code will display a message to the player, this time that they have received a mega shot bonus. The code is nearly the same as that for the game over message, except for a couple of details. The title of the message is set to "Bonus!" and a different message is displayed that is stored in the bonusMessage.

3.11 · Further Exploration

Your design game is finally finished. By completing this project you've learned about how physical interaction works in Unity, techniques for changing the view of a scene, how graphical interfaces are made and more. Hopefully this exercise has helped spark some ideas of your own for physics-

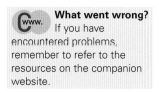

What went wrong? If you have encountered problems, remember to refer to the resources on the companion website.

based design games. Here are some possible directions for where you could take these ideas.

- In order to create very fine-grained, dense assemblages it would be necessary to have much smaller pieces of lumber. How would you go about accomplishing this?
- What if there were a 'bomb' object that the player could throw into the assemblage to separate the pieces from one another? A closer look at how the lumber gets "stuck", along with some research on the rigid body component may suggest an answer.
- Suppose Amanda from the Brief wanted to create these messy assemblages out of any arbitrary collection of items. By doing some research on the Unity website can you find out how you might replace the lumber objects in Slingshot with 3D models of other objects?

4

KIRIGAMI

4.1 · The Brief

John is an architect who has recently become interested in the art of kirigami. Unlike origami, the art of paper folding, kirigami allows cutting the paper in addition to folding. John has been exploring this art form to see how it might influence his architectural designs. He says that cutting and folding paper in a constrained manner offers him a novel way to model the envelope of buildings. The alternating opaque surfaces and voids that result from this process help him envision new designs. He has asked you to create a tool that allows him to play with these ideas. The software should present him with a blank sheet of paper and allow him to cut and fold it into a variety of forms. John appreciates the physical constraints of this art form and would like you to embed those same constraints into the software you build. He wants the experience to feel spontaneous and be a faster alternative to cutting and folding an actual sheet of paper.

4.2 · The Proposal

This design game will be simply called Kirigami, after the art form that inspired it. The first task will be to come up with a method for simulating a continuous piece of paper while allowing it to be cut and folded in a realistic manner. You will learn a method to accomplish this by using a grid of discrete elements connected together. This technique will result in a continuous looking sheet, but will allow separation between elements (cuts) as well as setting angles between elements (folds). Cutting can be defined relatively simply in this context as severing the connection between elements in the grid. Folding, however, is a bit more complex. You will need to create a mechanism by which John, our architect, can crease the paper in one direction or another and control the angle at which the paper creases. You will use a particularly useful physics component to meet this requirement.

In addition to the basic physical behavior of the simulated paper, you will build into this design game some extra constraints. These constraints will help achieve the spontaneous quality that John wants. Limitations on how many cuts and folds can be carried out will encourage thoughtful decisions. You'll build in mechanisms to make these limitations adjustable, so John can choose how constrained or free his designs will be. A timed mode will add another layer of constraint that will encourage quick thinking.

Finally, your design game will allow John to export the forms he creates. The exported models will be useful as he integrates his folded paper designs into the rest of his design processes.

4.3 · Opening the Project

Open the KirigamiStarter project found in the DesignGamesResources folder. Be sure that the MainScene is open by double-clicking on it in the Project View.

4.4 · The First Piece

In the Project view, take a look inside the Prefabs folder. Here you will find a 3D model named TriangleTile. Click on it and drag it into the Hierarchy View to copy it into the scene. You should see a white triangle appear in the Scene View.

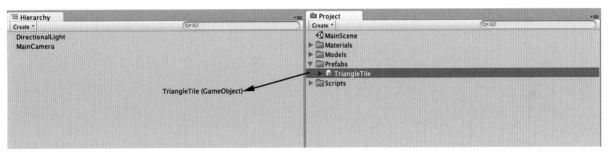

Fig. 4.1 Dragging the Triangle model into the Hierarchy View.

This triangle will form the basis for the simulated paper in this design game. When cutting and folding real paper, the number of possible actions that can be taken is infinite. The paper can be folded along any line, cut at any angle and combinations of these actions abound. For the purposes of Kirigami, you will be building 'paper' that behaves similarly, but limits the number of possible actions that can be taken. These limitations will help make coding more manageable while still allowing a wide variety of out-comes. In Kirigami, many of these triangles will be assembled into simulated sheets of paper that can be cut and folded.

By highlighting the TriangleTile in the Hierarchy View, you'll see in the Inspector that there are two extra components attached to it.

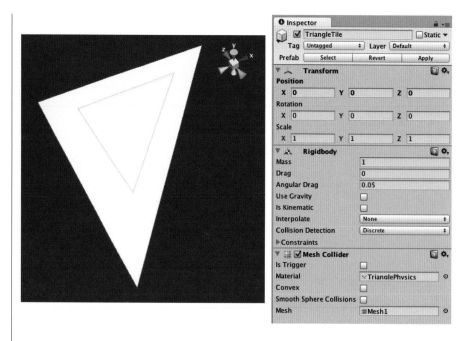

Fig. 4.2 A TriangleTile highlighted in the Scene View and the Inspector showing its components.

Recall from Chapter 3 that a rigid body is a component that allows objects to respond to physical forces such as gravity. This triangle has a rigid body that will ignore gravity, since the 'Use Gravity' parameter is false, but will respond to forces exerted on it from other triangles around it. Also attached to the triangle is a mesh collider. A collider, as you learned in the previous chapter, is a component that prevents objects from passing through one another. Here the collider, shown as a green outline in the Scene View, is slightly smaller than the overall dimensions of the triangle. You will see as this project progresses how this will allow the paper to bend and move without getting bound up at the edges of the triangles.

The triangle you have in your scene is only half of the picture. To create a sheet of paper, you will need a square tile that can be arrayed in a grid. To accomplish this, simply make a copy of the TriangleTile in the Hierarchy

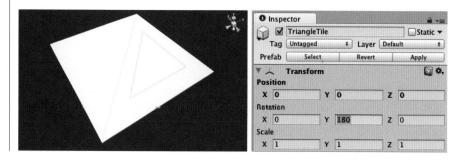

Fig. 4.3 Rotating the TriangleTile copy to form a square.

View by right-clicking on it and selecting Duplicate. With the copy highlighted in the Hierarchy View, change its y rotation to 180. This will spin the copy around so that it completes the square.

4.5 · The Joint

In order to assemble full sheets of paper out of this simple triangle, you will need to add some additional functionality to it. The component that will drive the majority of the behavior in the simulated paper is a joint. A joint is a component in Unity that behaves exactly like you would expect. Joints connect two objects together and constrain their movement in particular ways. They may be able to bend in relation to one another or spin around a common axis. They may be connected by a spring that allows them to be pulled apart, but always snap back together. You will be adding simple hinge joints to the triangles that will allow them to crease along their edges like paper.

To add the first hinge joint, highlight one of the TriangleTile objects in the Hierarchy View. In the Components menu, select **Physics > Hinge Joint**. You should see the new component appear in the Inspector.

Learn more about joints in the Chapter 4 section of the companion website.

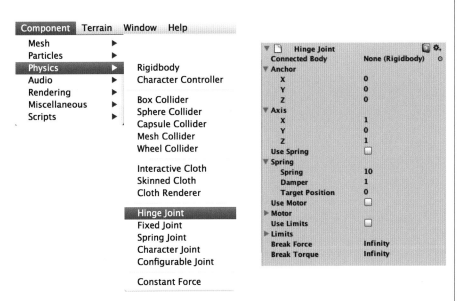

Notice that the hinge joint component has many parameters. Other joint types have even more of these settings. They allow the behavior of the joint to be tuned for specific situations. You will only need to change a few of these as they are shown in Figure 4.4. The axis of the hinge joint should

Fig. 4.4 Adding the Hinge Joint and the component as it looks in the Inspector.

be x = 1, y = 0, z = 1. This is the axis around which the two triangles will rotate. By default this is set to a vector pointing along the positive x axis. Since this joint will connect the two triangles along their diagonal sides, the axis needs to point along that line. The vector (1, 0, 1) does just that by defining a 45 degree angle.

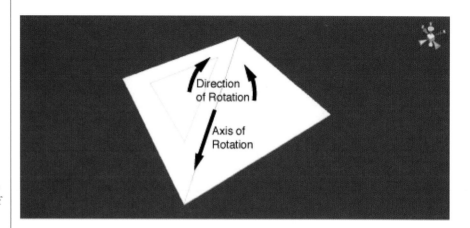

Fig. 4.5 Diagram showing the axis and direction of rotation of the hinge joint.

Another parameter that needs to be set is the spring parameter. In the Inspector, click on the checkbox next to Use Spring to enable this behavior. Immediately below, click the triangle next to Spring and enter 10 for Spring and 1 for Damper. These spring parameters allow the hinge joint to bounce back in a realistic way when the objects it connects are moved around. You will learn more about these settings as you progress.

The final step in defining this hinge joint is to specify a connected body. In the Hierarchy View, you should have one of the TriangleTile objects highlighted. This is the object that has the hinge joint component. You should also be able to see the hinge joint parameters, including Connected

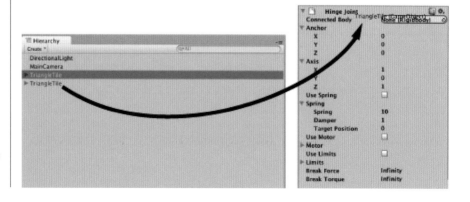

Fig. 4.6 Connecting the two triangles together by dragging the unhighlighted one onto the Connected Body line in the Inspector.

Body in the Inspector. To connect one triangle to the other, click and drag the TriangleTile that is not highlighted onto the Connected Body line in the Inspector. This maneuver can take some practice, as you may have noticed in previous chapters. If you have trouble, you can always try again.

4.6 · The Fold

Now that the two triangles of the square tile are connected with a hinge joint, they need to be able to fold. To enable this behavior, you'll need to add another object into the mix, along with some code. In the Prefabs folder found in the Project View, locate an object named JointIndicator. This object will serve as the primary means of interaction for the design game. It will be used to indicate where the simulated sheet of paper can be folded or cut. Drag a copy of this prefab into the Hierarchy View.

In the Scripts folder in the Project View you'll find the next piece of the puzzle. The JointController script will be the place where you will define the behavior for all of the joints, starting with the one you just created. Open the JointController script by double-clicking it in the Project View and add the following code.

Listing 4.1 Code to show and hide the JointIndicator in the JointController script (existing code in gray).

```
var triangleTile : Transform;
var jointIndex : int;
var jointToControl : HingeJoint;
var foldIncrement : float;

function Start ()
{
    renderer.enabled = false;
    var joints = triangleTile.GetComponents(HingeJoint);
    jointToControl = joints[jointIndex] as HingeJoint;
}

function Update ()
{

}

function OnMouseEnter ()
```

```
{
            renderer.enabled = true;
}

function OnMouseUp ()
{

}

function OnMouseExit ()
{
        renderer.enabled = false;
}
```

Starting at the top, this code defines a few variables that the script will use. You'll get to know the purpose of these variables as you write the code for Kirigami. In the Start function, the first line that you've written sets `renderer.enabled` to `false`. A renderer is a component that controls the appearance of an object; its materials, colors and other visual aspects. Here, `renderer` refers to the renderer component attached to the JointIndicator object. Setting the `enabled` property to false makes the object invisible when it is first created.

The next line of code creates a variable named `joints`. This variable is set equal to `triangleTile.GetComponents(HingeJoint)`; joints becomes a list of all of the HingeJoint components attached to the triangleTile object. So far there is only one HingeJoint attached to one of the triangles, so this list will only contain one item. As more joints are added, this list will grow. The final line in the Start function sets the variable `jointToControl` equal to `joints[jointIndex] as HingeJoint`. This code picks a HingeJoint from the `joints` list. When selecting a specific item from a list, square brackets ([ ]) are used along with a number called an index. The index number corresponds to the position in the list where the desired item is located. Since there is only one item in the list and index numbers start with zero, the `jointIndex` variable used here will be set to 0. This will specify the first, and so far only, joint in the list. You will set this variable in a bit, enabling this script to control the proper joint.

In the functions OnMouseEnter and OnMouseExit there are two similar lines of code. In the latter, renderer.enabled is set equal to true and in the former it is set to false. As you may already have guessed, this will make the JointIndicator object visible when the player positions the mouse cursor over it and invisible when they move the mouse cursor away from it.

Save the JointController script and return to Unity. Now you will attach the JointController script to the JointIndicator and set the variables that will make it operate. First, attach the script to the JointIndicator by dragging it from the Scripts folder in the Project View onto the JointIndicator in the Hierarchy. Highlight the JointIndicator in the Hierarchy and you should see the JointController script in the Inspector. Identify which of the TriangleTile objects in the Hierarchy has the HingeJoint attached. Making sure the JointIndicator is highlighted again, drag the TriangleTile over to the Inspector and drop it on the line in the JointController section labeled 'Triangle Tile'.

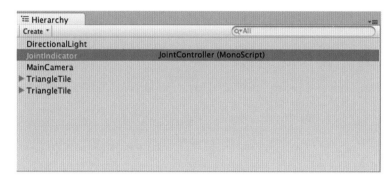

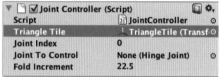

Fig. 4.7 Attaching the JointController script to the JointIndicator object (left) and modifying the parameters of the script in the Inspector (right).

Once the TriangleTile with the joint is connected to the script, check that the 'Joint Index' line is set to 0. This will ensure that this JointIndicator will be controlling the proper joint. The last parameter to set is 'Fold Increment'. Set this line to 22.5. You will use this number to determine how the triangles will fold.

Save your project and press play. You should be able to make the JointIndicator appear and disappear by moving your mouse cursor over the center of the white square and then away again. Showing and hiding the JointIndicator will give the player a way to know where they are able to fold the simulated paper you are creating.

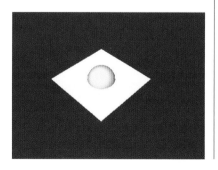

Fig. 4.8 JointIndicator hidden (left) and shown when the mouse cursor is over it (right).

95

The next addition to the JointController script will finally allow this tile to fold along its diagonal. You will use the JointIndicator object to accomplish this. Open, or return to, the JointController script and add the following line of code.

Listing 4.2 A single line of code added to the OnMouseUp function.

```
function OnMouseUp ()
{
    jointToControl.spring.targetPosition += foldIncrement;
}
```

Return to Unity and press play. Position your mouse over the center of the square tile and click. You should see the tile crease along its diagonal. If you repeat this, the fold angle should become increasingly more acute. The line of code that you added accomplishes this functionality in a very simple way. First, the OnMouseUp function is called whenever the player presses and then releases the mouse button while it's over the JointIndicator. Recall that the jointToControl variable refers to the HingeJoint on one of the TriangleTile objects. Here, you are accessing the spring component of this joint and setting its targetPosition to a new value. A spring component allows joints to move gradually toward a desired angle, as well as bounce back if they have exceeded that value. By adding (+=) the value foldIncrement to the spring's target position, you are instructing the joint to slowly move toward that new angle. Since the foldIncrement variable is currently set to 22.5 degrees, each time the mouse is clicked this joint will start moving toward a sharper angle.

You may have noticed if you clicked more than a couple of times that the JointIndicator sphere sinks deeper and deeper into the tiles. This is because, as the tiles change their positions, the JointIndicator stays in its original location. The final step in this section will correct this. In order to keep the sphere centered on the crease, one additional line of code is needed.

Listing 4.3 Tying the position of the JointIndicator to the TriangleTile object.

```
function Update ()
{
    transform.position =
    triangleTile.transform
    .TransformPoint( jointToControl.anchor );

}
```

This code sets the position of the JointIndicator equal to `triangleTile.transform.TransformPoint( jointToControl.anchor )`. The anchor property of the joint sets the joint's position relative to the object to which it's attached. The TransformPoint function finds the location of the anchor regardless of movement or rotation. Setting `transform.position` equal to this value will ensure that the indicator is always in the correct location. The joint attached to triangleTile is positioned at the origin (0, 0, 0) of the triangle, so here there is no modification of the indicator's position. As you move forward, this will not always be the case, which is why this code is included here. If you play the game again and click a few times, you should see the JointIndicator position itself at the center of the fold between the triangles.

Fig. 4.9 Two triangles folding incrementally with the JointIndicator positioned correctly.

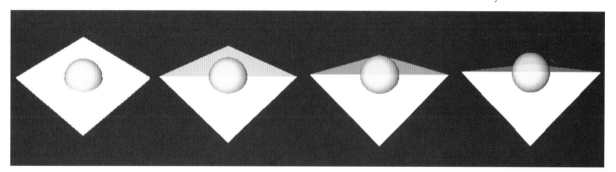

4.7 · Completing the Tile

Both triangles in the tile are connected with a hinge joint that can be manipulated by the player. The ultimate goal of this chapter is to create a large sheet of simulated paper, for which you will need to add a few more components. Starting with the two-triangle tile you have created, you will add two more joints and joint indicators to complete this square tile. Once this is done you will be able to assemble copies of the tile into larger sheets of foldable paper.

Drag the JointIndicator prefab from the Project View into the Hierarchy twice to make two new copies. These objects will each control one of the two new joints you just created. Highlight one at a time in the Hierarchy and, using the Inspector, set their positions to (0, 0, 0.5) and (−0.5, 0, 0). You'll notice that these points correspond to the locations of the two additional hinge joints. Both JointIndicator objects have the JointController script attached. You'll need to set the Triangle Tile and Joint Index parameters for each one. For both objects, drag the TriangleTile with the joints attached onto the Triangle Tile line in the Inspector. Remember that this line will be under the Joint Controller section in the Inspector when a JointIndicator is highlighted in the Hierarchy.

At this point there are multiple objects in the scene with the same name. To make things clearer and easier as you proceed it will help to give them more specific names. Rename the TriangleTile with the hinge joints 'JointedTriangle' and the other 'UnjointedTriangle'. The central JointIndicator should be renamed 'CenterIndicator'. Rename the JointIndicator with the anchor at (0, 0, −1) 'XIndicator' and the remaining JointIndicator 'ZIndicator'. These names will make coding much easier in the next sections.

With these pieces in place, you now have a complete square tile with three joints. To make it easier to make copies of this tile, you will need to package all of the objects up into a prefab. To do this, first create a new empty object by selecting **Game Object > Create Empty** from the main menu. Rename this object from 'GameObject' to 'PaperTile'. In the Project View, right-click on the Prefabs folder and select **Create > Prefab** from the menu. Rename this empty prefab from 'New Prefab' to 'PaperTile'. Now select the two TriangleTile objects (JointedTriangle and UnjointedTriangle), along with the three JointIndicator objects (CenterIndicator, XIndicator and ZIndicator). Drag everything onto the PaperTile object in the Hierarchy. Selecting multiple objects is accomplished by holding down the command (Mac) or control (Windows) key while clicking. This step is necessary because a prefab can only be created using a single object. With all of the pieces gathered together inside the PaperTile object, create the new prefab by dragging it onto the PaperTile prefab in the Project View. Your tile prefab is now ready to be duplicated. The final step in this section is to highlight the PaperTile prefab in the Project View and select 'Tile' from the tag dropdown menu at the top of the Inspector. This tag will help simplify the code in the next section.

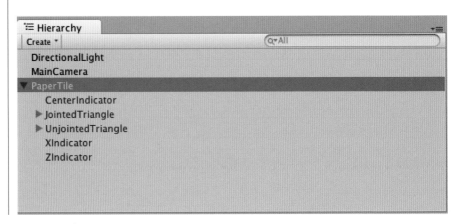

Fig. 4.10 Grouping all of the pieces together into the PaperTile object.

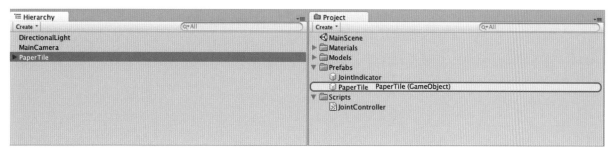

Fig. 4.11 Finishing the PaperTile prefab by dragging the PaperTile object to the Project View.

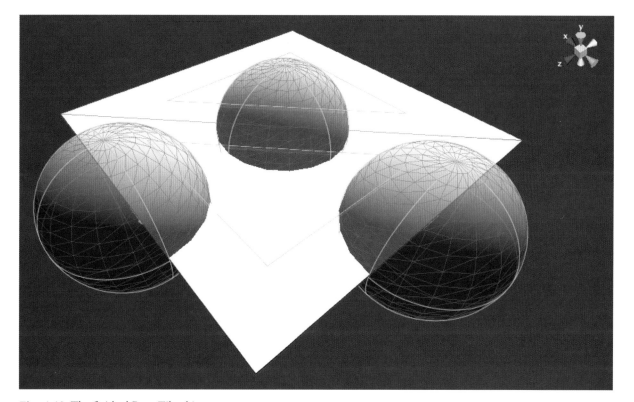

Fig. 4.12 The finished PaperTile object.

4.8 · Assembling the Paper

At this point you could start creating large sheets of paper by duplicating the PaperTile prefab and connecting the hinge joint of one tile to the next. Unfortunately, building up the paper manually, tile by tile, would be quite a bit of effort. The solution to this problem is to write some code that will automate the process. Open the PaperController script and add the following lines.

Listing 4.4 New code for the CreateSheet and DestroySheet functions in the PaperController script.

```
function CreateSheet ()
{
    for ( var i = 0; i < tileCountX; i++ )
    {
        for ( var j = 0; j < tileCountZ; j++ )
        {
            Instantiate( tilePrefab,
                        Vector3(
                        i - ( tileCountX * 0.5 ) - 0.5,
                        0,
                        j - ( tileCountZ * 0.5 ) - 0.5
                        ),
                        Quaternion.identity
                        );
        }
    }
}

function DestroySheet ()
{
    for ( var tile in
    GameObject.FindGameObjectsWithTag( "Tile" ) )
    {
        Destroy( tile );
    }
}
```

Inside the CreateSheet function there are two for loops. The first increments a variable i from zero up to `tileCountX`. The second, inner, loop increments a variable j up to `tileCountZ`. You can think about the first loop as counting through the columns of a grid and the second as counting through the rows. For instance, if both tileCountX and tileCountZ are set to five, this code will produce a five by five grid with a total of 25 tiles. The actual creation of the tiles happens with the `Instantiate` function inside the inner loop. Recall from previous chapters that Instantiate requires three pieces of data: an object to duplicate, a position and a rotation. Here the object to duplicate is specified by the tilePrefab which will be set to the PaperTile prefab in a bit. The position is a vector in which the x and z coordinates are calculated based on the values of i and j. In order to have the

For a refresher on how for loops work, refer to the Chapter 2 section of the companion website.

sheet of paper centered on the origin (0, 0, 0) the x coordinate is calculated by the expression i - (tileCountX * 0.5) - 0.5. If you assume a value of 5 for tileCountX, this means that the first tile that the loop creates will be positioned at −2. As the loop counts up, the tiles would be placed at −2, −1, 0, 1 and 2. The subtraction of 0.5 at the end of the expression takes into account the fact that the PaperTile is one unit wide, keeping the sheet centered at the origin.

The DestroySheet function uses a for loop as well. Here the loop is used to cycle through a list of all of the tiles in the scene. As opposed to the loops in the CreateSheet function which incremented a variable, this loop uses the 'for in' syntax. Loops using this syntax define a variable which will refer to each item in a list as the loop repeats. Take a look at the code `var tile in GameObject.FindObjectsWithTag( "Tile" )`. The first part defines a variable tile which will represent one specific PaperTile object at a time. The FindObjectsWithTag function collects all of the objects in the scene that have the tag "Tile". Inside the loop `Destroy( tile )` does exactly what you would expect: deletes the object referred to by the tile variable. When the DestroySheet function is called, all of the tiles will be deleted. Calling this function and then calling the CreateSheet function will have the effect of 'resetting' the sheet of paper. Save your script and your project and press play. Try clicking on a few joints to get a sense of how folding is working.

Fig. 4.13 Tiles folding along diagonal, but not along edges yet.

You should notice that only clicking on the center joints of the tiles has any real effect. This is because the tiles are not connected to one another yet. You'll fix this by adding a few more lines of code in the CreateSheet function of the PaperController script.

Listing 4.5 Adding another pair of loops to connect the tiles together.

```
function CreateSheet ()
{
    tiles = new GameObject[tileCountX, tileCountZ];
    for ( var i = 0; i < tiles.GetLength(0); i++ )
    {
        for ( var j = 0; j < tiles.GetLength(1); j++ )
        {
            tiles[i,j] = Instantiate( tilePrefab...
        }
    }
    for ( i = 0; i < tiles.GetLength(0); i++ )
    {
        for ( j = 0; j < tiles.GetLength(1); j++ )
        {
            var xcontroller =
            tiles[i,j].transform.Find( "XIndicator" )
            .GetComponent( JointController );
            if ( i == 0 )
            {
                xcontroller.DestroyJoint();
            } else {
                var xtarget = tiles[i - 1, j]
                .transform.Find( "UnjointedTriangle" );
                xcontroller.Connect( xtarget.rigidbody );
            }
            var zcontroller =
            tiles[i,j].transform.Find( "ZIndicator" )
            .GetComponent( JointController );
            if ( j == tiles.GetLength(1) - 1 )
            {
                zcontroller.DestroyJoint();
            } else {
                var ztarget = tiles[i, j + 1]
                .transform.Find( "UnjointedTriangle" );
                zcontroller.Connect( ztarget.rigidbody );
            }
        }
    }
}
```

At the top of the CreateSheet function, there is a new line the reads
`tiles = new GameObject[tileCountX, tileCountZ];`. It sets the value of

the tiles variable to a new empty array. Typically, arrays are simply lists of numbers, words or other data that can be cycled through using loops like the ones you've written. This array is a type known as a two-dimensional array. You can think of it like the squares on a chess board. The code new GameObject[tileCountX, tileCountZ] means that the objects that will be referred to by the array will be of the type GameObject and the size of the array will be 5 by 5, since these are the values currently stored in tileCountX and tileCountZ. This is like having a 5 by 5 square chess board, in which each square can hold a reference to an object. You will fill up this chess board with references to all of the PaperTile objects that make up the sheet of paper. Just before the word Instantiate, type in `tiles[i,j] = `, leaving the rest of the Instantiate line in place. This will store each PaperTile object in its own space in the array. Later in the CreateSheet function you'll be able to refer to the tiles by specifying their location on the grid. Since the variables i and j are counting through the columns and rows of the grid, tiles[0,0] will represent the first tile, tiles[0,1] the second, and so on.

Following the existing for loops you wrote previously, there are two more that reuse the variables i and j to cycle through the newly created tiles and connect them. You'll see that inside the loops there are two sections of code that look very similar. The first sets up some variables that start with x and the second with variables that start with z. These sections are responsible for connecting the negative x side of the tile and the positive z side, respectively. The first step in this task is to find the JointController script responsible for managing the joint that will connect the current tile to its neighbor. As the loops cycle through the tiles in the grid, the xcontroller variable is set equal to this script. The code `tiles[i,j].transform.Find("XIndicator")` locates the JointIndicator object on the negative x side of the current tile. Then `.GetComponent( JointController )` retrieves the script attached to it. All three of these lines, from var to the semicolon would usually be written on a single line. I've written them this way to help make the code readable. Either way works as well as the other.

Now that xcontroller can access the appropriate script, you'll use it to connect two adjacent tiles. The if statement that follows tests whether i is equal to 0 and, if it is, calls `xcontroller.DestroyJoint()`. You'll write this function in a bit, but its purpose is to delete the current JointIndicator. This is necessary since the first column of tiles will be on the edge of the sheet of paper. When i equals zero, it means that this code is currently going through the tiles in the first column, none of which will be connected on their negative x side. Deleting the JointIndicator on this side will avoid the confusion that would arise if the spherical indicators were present on the edge.

For all of the columns beyond the first, the `else` section of the if statement creates the necessary connection. A variable named `xtarget` is set equal to `tiles[i-1, j].transform.Find( "UnjointedTriangle" )`. This code finds the UnjointedTriangle object that is part of the neighboring tile. The neighboring tile is specified by tiles[i-1, j], since the joint on the negative x side of the current tile needs to connect with the tile in the previous column.

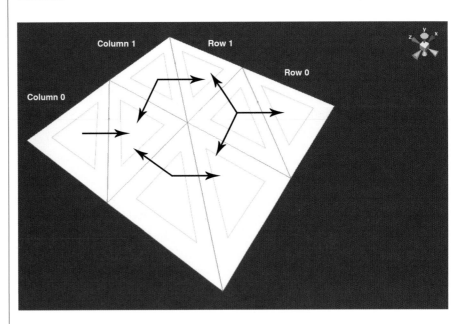

Fig. 4.14 Four tiles with arrows pointing from triangles with joints, to those with which they connect without joints.

Finally, `xcontroller.Connect( xtarget.rigidbody )` calls the Connect function in the JointController script to create the new hinge joint connection. It passes `xtarget.rigidbody` to the Connect function because joints can only connect one rigid body to another. The connect function will take this rigid body from the neighboring tile and link it together with the rigid body with which it is associated. You'll write the code for this function next. Open the JointController script and add the following code to the Connect function.

Listing 4.6 The Connect function in the JointController script.

```
function Connect (triangle : Rigidbody)
{
        jointToControl = triangleTile.AddComponent( HingeJoint );
```

```
    jointToControl.anchor = transform.localPosition;
    jointToControl.useSpring = true;
    jointToControl.spring.spring = 10.0;
    jointToControl.spring.damper = 1.0;
    if ( gameObject.name == "XIndicator" )
    {
        jointToControl.axis = Vector3( 0, 0, -1 );
    }
    if ( gameObject.name == "ZIndicator" )
    {
        jointToControl.axis = Vector3( -1, 0, 0 );
    }
    jointToControl.connectedBody = triangle;
}
```

Inside the parentheses that follow `function Connect`, you'll see `triangle : Rigidbody`. This indicates that this function requires a rigid body in order to do its work. You've already accomplished this by passing one when you called this function from the PaperController script. The first thing the function does is set `jointToControl` equal to `triangleTile.AddComponent( HingeJoint )`. Recall that the triangleTile variable refers to the triangle with which this JointIndicator is associated. The AddComponent function here creates a new hinge joint and attaches it to triangleTile. From now on, jointToControl will refer to this new joint.

The next few lines set the parameters of the new hinge joint. These correspond to the same settings you used when you created the joint that linked the two triangles of a tile together. The `anchor` parameter sets the location of the joint relative to the object to which it's attached. The value for anchor is set to `transform.localPosition`, which is the JointIndicator's position relative to the PaperTile as a whole. While transform.position would give this object's location relative to the origin of the scene, localPosition gives the location relative to the object that contains it. This ensures that the joint will be positioned halfway along the edge of the triangle, just like the JointIndicator.

The useSpring, spring.spring and spring.damper parameters are all given the same values as the center joint. Setting the `useSpring` parameter to `true` means that the joint will move in a gradual manner. The `spring.spring` parameter is set to `10`, which tells the joint to move towards its target angle quickly. With the `spring.damper` parameter at a value of `1`, this joint will have a bit of bounce when it folds past its target angle.

Next, there are two if statements that check the name of the JointIndicator. If the name is "XIndicator" the axis of the jointToContol is set to Vector3(0, 0, -1). If the name is "ZIndicator" the axis is set to Vector3(-1, 0, 0). This axis vector, as you've seen before, determines how the hinge joint will rotate. These values ensure the rotation of all of the joints will be consistent. The final line in the Connect function sets joint-ToControl.connectBody equal to triangle. The connectedBody of a joint is the rigid body to which it's connected. Here, you are specifying the rigid body of the neighboring triangle, referred to by the triangle variable you passed to the function.

You are almost ready to test out your foldable sheet of paper. The next few modifications to the JointController script will get you there.

Listing 4.7 The DestroyJoint function in the JointController script.

```
function DestroyJoint ()
{
    if ( jointToControl != null )
    {
        Destroy( jointToControl );
    }
    Destroy( gameObject );
}
```

Adding the code above will allow for the deletion of those joints at the edges of the paper. First, if jointToControl != null tests whether there is already a joint attached and if so deletes it with Destroy(jointToControl. Next the JointIndicator that this script is attached to deletes itself with Destroy(gameObject).

Listing 4.8 Updated Start and Update functions for the JointController script.

```
function Start ()
{
    renderer.enabled = false;
    if ( gameObject.name == "CenterIndicator" )
    {
        jointToControl =
        triangleTile.GetComponent( HingeJoint );
    }
}
```

```
function Update ()
{
    if ( jointToControl != null )
    {
        transform.position =
        triangleTile.transform
        .TransformPoint( jointToControl.anchor );

    }
}
```

The last piece of the puzzle is to modify the Start and Update functions so they cooperate with the new functionality of the design game. The added if statement in the Start function ensures that only the center JointIndicator will take ownership of the first hinge joint linking the two triangles of the tile. The if statement in Update checks to make sure there is a joint present before it tries to move the indicator.

With these changes made, you're ready to save everything, press play and test out the paper you've created. Be sure to click on a variety of joints. Click on the Show Menu button, then the New Sheet button to start again. Try folding the paper in half along a line of your choosing.

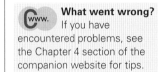

What went wrong? If you have encountered problems, see the Chapter 4 section of the companion website for tips.

Fig. 4.15 A folded sheet of simulated paper.

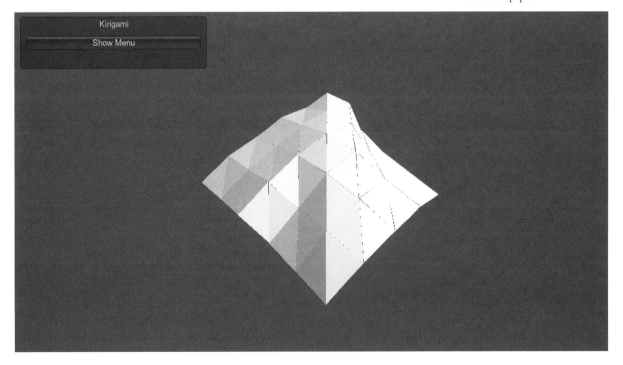

4.9 · The Counter Fold

When you click on the joints of the paper they fold, but so far only in one direction. To allow the player greater freedom to create, you will need to provide a way to enable folding in the opposite direction. This can be accomplished with just a few lines of code, as shown below.

Listing 4.9 Updated OnMouseEnter and OnMouseUp functions in the JointController script.

```
function OnMouseEnter ()
{
    renderer.enabled = true;
    if ( Input.GetKey(KeyCode.LeftShift) ||
        Input.GetKey(KeyCode.RightShift) )
    {
        renderer.material.color = Color.green;
    } else {
        renderer.material.color = Color.yellow;
    }
}

function OnMouseUp ()
{
    if ( Input.GetKey(KeyCode.LeftShift) ||
        Input.GetKey(KeyCode.RightShift) )
    {
        jointToControl.spring.targetPosition -= foldIncrement;
    } else {
        jointToControl.spring.targetPosition += foldIncrement;
    }
}
```

The OnMouseEnter function gets called when the player moves the mouse cursor over the JointIndicator. The if statement inside the function tests whether the player is pressing the shift key using `Input.GetKey(KeyCode.LeftShift)` and `Input.GetKey(KeyCode.RightShift)`. The Input.GetKey function is true whenever the key specified is pressed down and false when it's not. The double pipe symbol (||) can be read as the word 'or'. If the shift key is down, the line `renderer.material.color = Color.green` changes the color of the JointIndicator to green. When the shift key isn't pressed, the color is set to yellow as it was originally. The color change will indicate to the player in which direction the sheet will fold.

OnMouseUp contains the exact same if statement. Here it controls whether to reduce or increase the target angle of the joint. When the shift key is held down `foldIncrement` is subtracted from `jointToControl.spring.targetPosition`. This causes the joint to fold in the opposite direction relative to the original behavior which you defined before which added this value to the target. This is all the code necessary to enable the two fold directions. Save and press play to see it in action.

Fig. 4.16 The indicator: yellow normally and green with the shift key held down.

4.10 · The Cut

As you've proceeded through the chapters of this book, you've probably noticed that as the exercises progress it takes less and less code to enable the next bit of functionality. This is one of the joys of learning to code. At first there is a great deal of code to write and it produces very little in the way of visible results. This foundational code sets the ground work for later code, allowing it to do a great deal in a few lines. Adding the cutting functionality outlined in the first section of this chapter will reinforce this.

Listing 4.10 The two additions to the if statements in OnMouseEnter and OnMouseUp that enable cutting of the paper.

```
function OnMouseEnter ()
{
    renderer.enabled = true;
    if ( Input.GetKey(KeyCode.LeftShift) ||
    Input.GetKey(KeyCode.RightShift) )
    {
        renderer.material.color = Color.green;
```

```
    } else if ( Input.GetKey(KeyCode.LeftControl) ||
            Input.GetKey(KeyCode.RightControl) ) {
        renderer.material.color = Color.red;
    } else {
        renderer.material.color = Color.yellow;
    }
}

function OnMouseUp ()
{
    if ( Input.GetKey(KeyCode.LeftShift) ||
    Input.GetKey(KeyCode.RightShift) )
    {
        jointToControl.spring.targetPosition -= foldIncrement;
    } else if ( Input.GetKey(KeyCode.LeftControl) ||
            Input.GetKey(KeyCode.RightControl) ) {
        DestroyJoint();
    } else {
        jointToControl.spring.targetPosition += foldIncrement;
    }
}
```

The code above enables the paper to be cut in just a few lines. The `else if` statement is a way to add another condition to an if statement. Many of these statements can be added to an if statement in order to test for many different scenarios that may occur as the state of a game changes. The two you've added to the OnMouseEnter and OnMouseUp functions

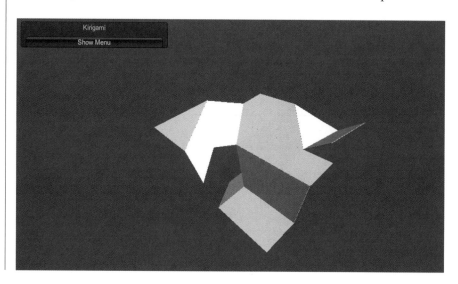

Fig. 4.17 A sheet both cut and folded.

test for whether the control key (`KeyCode.LeftControl` or `KeyCode.RightControl`) is being held down. When the mouse cursor is positioned over a JointIndicator and the control key is down, the indicator's color is changed to red. If the player then presses and releases the mouse button the `DestroyJoint` function is called, breaking the link between the two neighboring tiles.

Give it a try. When you play the design game you should now be able to fold in two directions and cut the sheet of paper along any seam. Generate a fresh sheet whenever you want. See what you can create.

4.11 · More or Less

Thus far, unless you have changed the tile count variables, your sheet of paper has consisted of five by five tiles. To offer the player even more freedom, and perhaps complication, you can allow them to change the size of the sheet. You can do this by giving the player a way to change the tile count variables. In the OnGUI function of the PaperController script, add the following code.

Listing 4.11 Adding some sliders to the OnGUI function to control the size of the sheet.

```
if ( GUILayout.Button( "Hide Menu" ) )
{
    showMenu = false;
}
GUILayout.BeginHorizontal();
GUILayout.Label("Sheet Width (" + tileCountX + "): ");
tileCountX = GUILayout.HorizontalSlider(
            tileCountX, 5.0, 20.0 );
GUILayout.EndHorizontal();
GUILayout.BeginHorizontal();
GUILayout.Label("Sheet Depth (" + tileCountZ + "): ");
tileCountZ = GUILayout.HorizontalSlider(
            tileCountZ, 5.0, 20.0 );
GUILayout.EndHorizontal();
if ( GUILayout.Button( "New Sheet" ) )
{
    DestroySheet();
    CreateSheet();
}
```

The `GUILayout.BeginHorizontal` and `GUILayout.EndHorizontal` functions define areas in which user interface elements are laid out left to right. With each pair of these functions there are two interface elements. `GUILayout.Label` simply puts some text on the screen. In this case, it is displaying the text "Sheet Width" and "Sheet Depth" along with the current x and z dimensions of the sheet in parentheses. GUILayout.HorizontalSlider requires three pieces of data: a variable that establishes the current position of the slider, a minimum value and a maximum value. For the x dimension, these values are `tileCountX, 5.0, 20.0`. The tileCountX = at the start of this line means that when the player moves the slider, the resultant value will be stored in tileCountX, changing the text in the label and the starting value of the slider in the next frame. Try playing the game, clicking the Show Menu button and adjusting the sliders you've added.

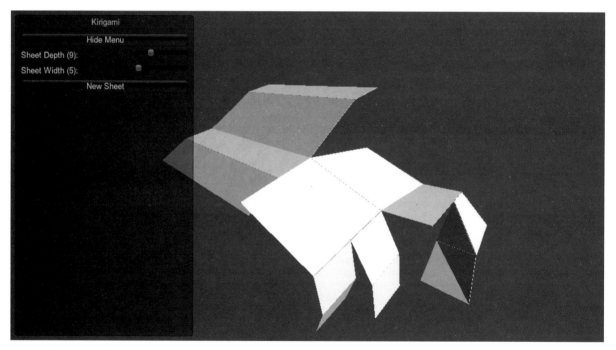

Fig. 4.18 Newly added sliders adjusting the size of the sheet.

While allowing this change of size was easy enough, it raises a new problem. If the sheet gets too big, it will no longer be entirely visible to the camera. I've provided you with a solution to this challenge. Locate the CameraController script in the Project View and drag it onto MainCamera in the Hierarchy to attach it. This script works similarly to the camera movement code you wrote in the previous chapter. It allows the player to rotate the view by dragging with the right mouse button held down. It also allows zooming in and out via the scroll wheel. With this script in place the player will be able to adjust their vantage point to see the entire sheet or to get in close for precise cutting and folding. Save the project and try this out for yourself.

4.12 · Exercising Constraint

In this section you will add the type of constraints that were outlined in the first sections of this chapter. The player will have the option at the start of each game to select the size of the sheet of paper, a time limit and a limit on how many cuts and folds can be carried out. The first bit of code goes in the Update function of the PaperController script.

Listing 4.12 Code to keep track of time in the Update function of the PaperController script.

```
function Update ()
{
    if ( !startMode && !gameOver && timerEnabled )
    {
        gameTimer -= Time.deltaTime;
        if ( gameTimer <= 0 )
        {
            gameTimer = 0.0;
            gameOver = true;
        }
    }
}
```

The first if statement in the Update function checks the state of three variables. The startMode variable will be true if the player hasn't begun playing yet. An exclamation point (!) indicates that this variable should be false for the code inside the if statement to execute. The gameOver variable will be true once the player has run out of time or has used up all of their cutting and folding opportunities. Since this code manages the game timer, gameOver should be false for the clock to be counting down. Lastly the timerEnabled variable should be true. The player determines this when they start a game. Recall that the && symbol means that all of these variables need to have the correct values if the code inside is to run.

During each frame `Time.deltaTime`, the amount of time that has elapsed since the previous frame, is subtracted from the `gameTimer` variable. An if statement then checks to see if gameTimer is less than or equal (<=) to zero. If it is, `gameOver` is set to `true`, setting off the end of the game.

Next, add the following code to the StartGame, PlayAgain and CountCutOrFold functions.

Listing 4.13 StartGame, PlayAgain and CountCutOrFold functions.

```
function StartGame()
{
    CreateSheet();
    gameTimer = timeLimit;
    cutFoldCount = 0;
    startMode = false;
    showMenu = true;
}


function PlayAgain()
{
    DestroySheet();
    startMode = true;
    gameOver = false;
}


function CountCutOrFold ()
{
    cutFoldCount++;
    if ( cutFoldCount >= cutFoldLimit )
    {
        gameOver = true;
    }
}
```

StartGame will now be responsible for generating a new sheet of paper at the beginning of a game using the `CreateSheet` function. Because of this, you should at this point scroll up to the Start function of the script and remove the line that calls CreateSheet. It also resets the variables `gameTimer`, `start-Mode` and `showMenu` to their proper values.

The PlayAgain function cleans up at the end of a game. `DestroySheet` deletes all of the paper tiles present in the scene. It sets `startMode` to `true` so the player will be able to make their choices for the next game. It also sets gameOver to false, allowing a new game to begin.

CountCutOrFold keeps track of how many operations the player has carried out on the sheet of paper. First, cutFoldCount++ adds one to this variable that tracks the total number of cuts or folds. Then an if statement checks to see if cutFoldCount is at or above (>=) the cutFoldLimit value set by the player. If it is, gameOver becomes true, ending the game.

The CountCutOrFold function needs to be called whenever the player clicks on a JointIndicator object. One line of code takes care of this task in the JointController script.

Listing 4.14 Using the SendMessage function: the OnMouseUp function of the JointController script.

```
} else {
        jointToControl.spring.targetPosition += foldIncrement;
    }
    GameObject.Find( "MainCamera" )
    .SendMessage( "CountCutOrFold" );
}
```

Here GameObject.Find("MainCamera") gets a reference to the MainCamera object that has the PaperController script attached to it. The SendMessage function will call the specified function on any script attached to MainCamera. In this case it will call CountCutOrFold in the PaperController script to keep a running total of the operations carried out on the sheet.

The next step is to give the player a way to adjust all of the variables you've seen in this section. In the OnGUI function of the PaperController script, you may have already noticed a large amount of code that shows up as green in the editor. This code has been commented out, or disabled, by the symbols /* and */. Look through the code and locate the four lines where these symbols appear and remove them. This will enable new graphical elements that the player will use to set up the constraints of their game of Kirigami. The code in the OnGUI function should look familiar based on your experience in the previous chapter, but take a look through it to make sure you can tell what it's doing.

The final task in this section is to return to Unity, highlight the MainCamera in the Hierarchy and check the box next to 'Start Mode' in

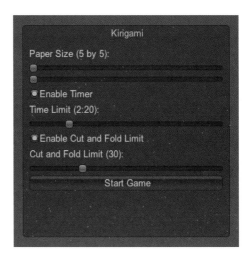

Fig. 4.19 The new start screen for Kirigami.

the Inspector. If you press play you should now see a box with sliders and buttons with which you can configure the constraints of the game.

4.13 · Big Finish

Play a game through to the end by enabling the time limit, the cut and fold limit or by clicking the 'Done!' button. Code in the OnGUI function will show a game over screen with the option to play again or export a model.

Fig. 4.20 Game over screen.

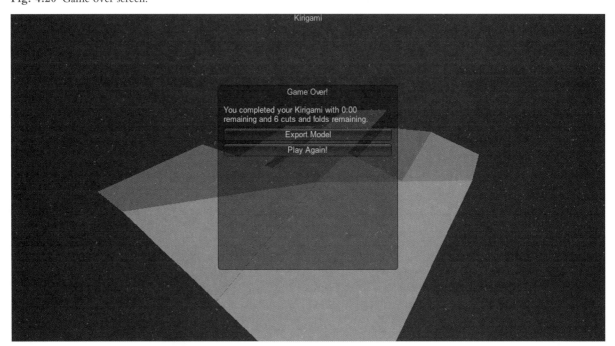

The export model button will take the geometrical data of each of the paper tiles and write it out in a 3D model format called OBJ. This format is quite basic and has been around for quite some time. You can open OBJ files in a variety of 3D modeling programs. The exported file can be located in the same folder where your Unity project is saved. To achieve this functionality, I modified some code that was written by Keli Hlodversson and posted on the Unity wiki. There are many Unity users who contribute code like this to the community. You can find other examples on the various support websites as well as the Asset Store, which you can access by selecting **Window > Asset Store** from the main menu in Unity.

The Asset Store has a wide variety of scripts, materials and 3D models that you can incorporate into your projects.

4.14 · Further Exploration

Congratulations on completing yet another design game. You've probably already started to think about ways to modify and improve Kirigami. Here are a few suggestions to get you thinking about the possibilities.

* Suppose our architect friend John from the Brief wanted to be able to fold and cut the paper at a smaller scale. How might you achieve this functionality?
* Clicking each joint indicator to either fold or cut works just fine, but suppose you wanted the player to be able to fold along the entire length of the paper in one move. What kind of code would you write to allow dragging the mouse across the sheet to fold or cut? Take a look at the OnMouseUp function in the JointController script, then try to find an alternative function that would work differently.
* Think of shapes other than triangles that you could use in combination with joints that would create an entirely different experience for the player. A good example can be found in a certain multi-colored, rotating cube popular in the 1980s.

5

COMPONENT
LAB

5.1 · The Brief

Jessica is an architect who has recently become very interested in the field of chemistry. After reading several books on the subject she started seeing many similarities between the logic of assembling a building and that of molecules that form bonds among themselves. She has come to understand that the forces that govern the very small world of chemistry have analogies in the very large world of architecture. At the heart of both worlds is a fundamental reliance on the geometry of components to enable stable structures to be formed.

A very interesting aspect of molecular bonding from Jessica's point of view is its automatic nature. When a negatively charged part of one molecule gets close enough to a positively charged part of another the two instantly form a strong bond and start functioning as a single unit. Jessica has been wondering whether it would be possible to simulate the same sort of automated assembly using pieces less like molecules and more like architectural components. She's thinking of a kind of virtual beaker that could be filled with a variety of 3D shapes that she could stir up and see them aggregate together like in a chemistry experiment. Her intuition is that this sort of a tool would be a way to 'grow' new types of structures that she hasn't thought of before.

5.2 · The Proposal

Building Jessica's virtual chemistry experiment will require a few decisions to be made. The first is to figure out what sort of components this design game will need. Should they be very simple, like in a toy construction set, or should they be more complex, modeled after actual architectural building components? For the purposes of this chapter you will start with a variety of basic components that have the potential to aggregate into interesting structures. This will simplify the process of developing the design game and will make it easier to arrive at a proof of concept. Once you have verified that this concept works with a simple kit of parts, you can better envision how it could evolve to handle more complicated scenarios.

The logic of how the components will bond to each other will be the big challenge of this endeavor. There are many ways to link objects together in Unity such as the joint components you explored in Chapter 4. For Component Lab, you will write code that will imbue each component with simple intelligence, enabling them to make decisions about how and when to form bonds. It is also worth considering whether the player can intervene and break those bonds apart. This will require you to learn a bit more about 3D geometry, movement and managing the state of objects. This behavior will get built up piece by piece until this chemistry set is fully operational.

Finally, there is the question of productive constraints and what does it mean to 'win' at this design game. Constraints could include time limits as you've explored before, but Component Lab seems less suited for this. More appropriate constraints might include limiting the number or variety of components, or the size of the virtual container in which they bond together. Closely related to these constraints is the task of evaluating how well the player is doing in the game. They could be evaluated based on the overall size of the assembly they achieve or the total number of components in the assemblage. The ratio of those components that make bonds versus those that don't could also be a factor. You'll explore these and several other challenges as you work through this chapter.

5.3 · Opening the Project

Open the ComponentLabStarter project in Unity. Take a survey of the various models, scripts and other items in the Project View. You'll be using each of these in turn as the chapter progresses. Double-click on the MainScene in the Project View to ensure it's the scene you are editing.

5.4 · Setting the Stage

There will need to be a place in which the components will interact with one another; a 'virtual beaker' as Jessica called it in the Brief. I've created this beaker for you. Find it in the Project View under the Prefabs folder and drag

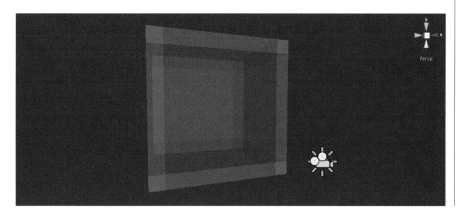

Fig. 5.1 The beaker container added to the scene.

it into the Hierarchy to create a copy. Highlight the Beaker in the Hierarchy and set its position to (0, 0, 0) using the Inspector.

If you examine the beaker and its various parts it should look familiar. It's constructed very similarly to the play box from the Slingshot project, except with six cubes forming the sides of an enclosed box. For the beaker, I've applied some materials which give the sides their translucent blue color. This will allow players to see what's going on inside, but still understand where the boundaries of the beaker are. This box will be where all of the action in Component Lab will take place.

I've provided a CameraController script that is attached to the MainCamera object. You can press play to see how it works. By right-clicking and dragging across the screen you can orbit around the beaker. If you hold down the shift key while dragging you can pan the camera up, down and side to side. If you scroll up or down, the camera will move closer in or further out. This functionality will allow the player to get a better look at specific areas of interest as events play out.

There is also a GameController script attached to the MainCamera. Inside, there is some code to show or hide the beaker. With the MainCamera highlighted in the Hierarchy, drag the Beaker object over to the Beaker line in the Inspector. This will allow the beaker to be shown or hidden when the B key is pressed. Hiding the beaker will enable the player to get an even better look without the walls of the beaker obscuring their view.

5.5 · The First Component

Locate an object named RoundedBar in the Project View. You'll find it inside the Models folder. Drag it into the Hierarchy to make a copy, then position your mouse over the Scene View and press the F key to zoom in on the new object. This bar with rounded ends will form the basis of your first intelligent component.

Keep the RoundedBar highlighted in the Hierarchy and click on the triangle icon next to its name. This will display 'Mesh 1' directly beneath the RoundedBar line. This mesh object contains all of the 3D data necessary to render the object. You'll need to enable the RoundedBar to respond to physical forces, for which you'll need two components. First, add a collider by selecting **Component > Physics > Box Collider** from the main menu. In the Inspector you will see the Box Collider component along with its various parameters. Just one of the Material parameters will need changing.

Locate the ComponentPhysics material in the Materials folder of the Project View and drag it to the Material line in the Inspector. This material contains data on how this object will move, bounce and collide with other objects.

The second component that needs to be added to the RoundedBar is a rigid body. Recall that a rigid body is necessary for an object to have mass, to move in response to forces and react to collisions. Select **Component > Physics > Rigidbody** from the main menu to add one. No further configuration is necessary; the rigid body is ready to go. The RoundedBar is now a fully physical object.

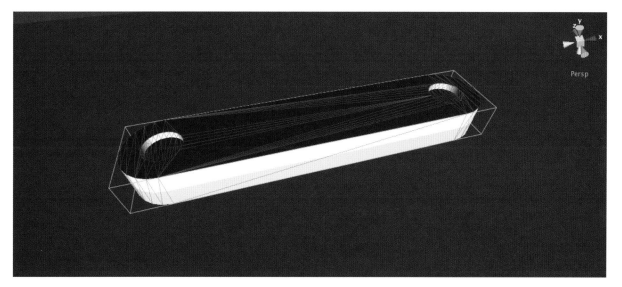

Fig. 5.2 The RoundedBar object with a collider and rigid body attached.

If you take a closer look, you'll see four circular indentations on the RoundedBar. These will be the locations where joints will be placed when components bond. You made extensive use of hinge joints in the previous chapter. Component Lab will use them again, along with other types of joints to enable components to bond to one another. With RoundedBar still highlighted in the Hierarchy, find a script named ComponentController in the Project View under the scripts folder. Drag this script onto the RoundedBar in the Hierarchy to attach it. This script will be where you will define the behavior that allows components to bond to each other.

The ComponentController script has a variable named bondingPoints that governs how joints are created. Whereas most lists you would create are made up of a single type of data, say Vector3 objects or floats, this list is made up of objects of a type called BondingPoint. If you open up the

ComponentController script you will see the definition of this new type towards the top of the file. It starts with `public class BondingPoint`. You can think of a class as a template from which data objects can be created, each with different values stored in their parameters. Other types that you have been using such as GameObject, HingeJoint, and all the others also have classes from which unique data objects – or instances – are made. It's not important right now that you understand how classes work. If you continue exploring programming beyond this book, you will certainly learn a lot more about this topic.

With the RoundedBar highlighted in the Hierarchy, locate the Bonding Points list in the Inspector. If you click the triangle icon at the start of the line, you should see a line with the label Size appear directly under the parameter names. Change the size of the list by typing 4 into the Size line. Add the data to the Bonding Points list as shown in Table 5.1. The Joint Position, Joint Axis and Joint Type parameters need to be set for each element in the list. Leave the other parameters under each element with their original values.

Table 5.1 Parameter values for the four BondingPoint data objects in the Bonding Points list.

List Element	Joint Position	Joint Axis	Joint Type	Bond Set
Element 0	(0.4, 0.05, 0)	(0, 1, 0)	Hinge	1
Element 1	(−0.4, 0.05, 0)	(0, 1, 0)	Hinge	1
Element 2	(0.4, −0.05, 0)	(0, −1, 0)	Hinge	2
Element 3	(−0.4, −0.05, 0)	(0, −1, 0)	Hinge	2

With the data input into the Bonding Points list, the RoundedBar now has all of the information it will need to create up to four hinge joints. Each of the joints will be centered on the indentations in the bar with their axes pointed away from the surface. You will make use of this data in the next section when you define the behavior of this component.

Lastly make this component into a prefab so it can be easily copied. In the Project View, right-click on the Prefabs folder and select **Create > Prefab** from the menu. Rename this new prefab RoundedBar. Then drag the RoundedBar from the Hierarchy onto the new prefab. Select the prefab and, in the Inspector, select the "Component" tag in the tag dropdown menu. This tag will help with writing code to find all of the components in the scene. You can now delete the RoundedBar object from the Hierarchy by right-clicking on it and selecting **Delete** from the menu. From now on new copies of this component will be created from the prefab.

5.6 · Creating Components

Now you can define how components will be added to the beaker. The first step will be to add the component to a list in the GameController script. Highlight the MainCamera in the Hierarchy and look for the GameController script in the Inspector. Under Component Prefabs you should see a line labeled Size. Click the triangle icon at the start of the line if Size isn't visible. If you change the value of Size to 1, you should see another line appear labeled Element 0. Drag the RoundedBar from the Project View onto this line to add it to the list. The Component Prefabs list will enable the GameController script to know which prefab components are available for use. You will refer to this list frequently as you progress.

Perform a similar action with the Component Icons list. Change the size of this list to 1. Drag the RoundedBarIcon image from the Textures folder in the Project View onto the Element 0 line. This list will be used to create buttons for each of the component prefabs you add to the project.

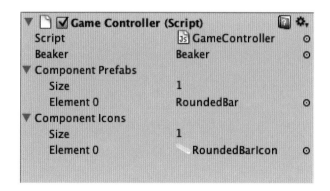

Fig. 5.3 RoundedBar prefab added to the Component Prefabs list and the RoundedBarIcon added to the Component Icons list.

With these parameters defined, you can open the GameController script and add some code that will drop components into the beaker.

Listing 5.1 The CreateComponents function in the GameController script.

```
function CreateComponents ( component_index : int )
{
    for ( var i = 0; i < numberOfComponentsToCreate; i++ )
```

```
    {
        var component_location = Vector3(
        Random.Range(  creationArea.min.x,
                       creationArea.max.x ),
        Random.Range(  creationArea.min.y,
                       creationArea.max.y ),
        Random.Range(  creationArea.min.z,
                       creationArea.max.z ) );
        Instantiate( componentPrefabs[component_index],
        component_location, Quaternion.identity );
    }
}
```

The CreateComponents function consists of a loop that counts up from 0 to numberOfComponentsToCreate, a variable that the player will adjust using the menu created in the OnGUI function. For each count up, the function creates a vector named component_location that will serve as the initial position of a new component. The vector is created by using Random.Range three times to arrive at random values for the x, y and z coordinates. Recall from previous projects that Random.Range needs two pieces of data, a minimum amount and a maximum amount. Here these values come from creationArea, a Bounds object that forms an invisible volume inside the beaker. Using the minimum and maximum values from this volume guarantees that the initial positions of new components will be directly within the beaker, preventing them from falling outside it. For example, Random.Range(creationArea.min.x, creationArea.max.x) will choose an x value for the component's position that is between the farthest left and farthest right edges of the creationArea volume. The size and position of creationArea can be changed in the Inspector when the MainCamera is highlighted.

Following the creation of the component_location vector, the Instantiate function creates a copy of the chosen component referred to by componentPrefabs[i], then positions it at component_location. The specific component to create is chosen by the player in the game menu. This code is already in place inside the OnGUI function.

Listing 5.2 The existing code in the OnGUI function that calls the CreateComponents function.

```
if ( GUILayout.Button(   componentIcons[i],
                         GUILayout.Width(64),
                         GUILayout.Height(64) ) )
```

```
{
    CreateComponents( i );
}
```

The OnGUI function creates a set of buttons, one for each of the images in the componentIcons list. The code above monitors these buttons and, if one of them is clicked, calls the CreateComponents function you just wrote.

Save the GameController script and try creating some components. In the menu on the left side of the screen, move the slider to adjust the number to create, then click the button with the image of the RoundedBar on it. You should see several RoundedBar objects appear in the beaker. Adjust the number to create again with the slider and verify that you can add a lot of components at one time. Being able to adjust the amount of components that are added to the beaker will allow the player to fine-tune how components combine, and in what ratios.

Play the game and verify that components are getting created. Do this by clicking on the button with the image of the RoundedBar component on it.

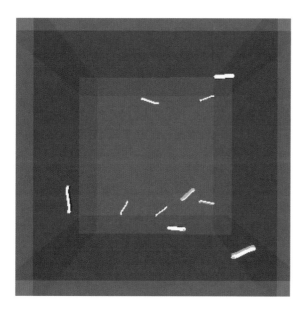

Fig. 5.4 Components created in the beaker.

5.7 · The Management

In order for all of the components in this simulation to behave correctly there needs to be a boss in charge of who does what, and when they do it. If all of the components scrambled to bond at the same time the result would be a chaotic mess. Next you will add two sets of functions to the GameController script that will help manage the bonding process.

Listing 5.3 The GetNewGroupNumber and MergeGroups functions of the GameController script.

```
function GetNewGroupNumber () : int
{
    componentGroupCounter++;
    return componentGroupCounter;
}

function MergeGroups ( g1 : int, g2 : int )
{
    for ( var component : GameObject in
        GameObject.FindGameObjectsWithTag( "Component" ) )
    {
        if ( component
            .GetComponent( ComponentController )
            .group == g2 )
        {
            component
            .GetComponent( ComponentController ).group = g1;
        }
    }
}
```

The GetNewGroupNumber function above is very simple, but essential to the operation of this design game. As components bond with each other, they will form large, interconnected masses. If two components in the same mass tried to connect, they will most likely be unable because of geometrical constraints. This function hands out unique group numbers. This allows components to know that they shouldn't try to bond with one another if they are in the same group. First the function adds one to a variable using `componentGroupCounter++`. It then hands that number back to the component that asked for it with `return componentGroupCounter`. Notice that you need to add `: int` after the parentheses of this function. You can read this as 'returns this type of data'. Since this function returns an integer, int is specified as the type after the colon.

The second function in this pair, MergeGroups, handles the case in which two groups of components join together. When this happens, each group has its own unique number. When combined into a single aggregation, they need to know which of those numbers to use for the new, larger group. The g1 and g2 arguments inside the parentheses after the function name will specify which two groups are joining.

The for loop inside the function gathers a list of all of the components in the scene using `GameObject.FindGameObjectsWithTag( "Component" )`. Each component that the for loop looks at will be referred to by the `component` variable declared inside the parentheses. For each component, an if statement tests whether its `group` number matches the number contained in the `g2` variable. If this is the case, the code inside simply changes that component's group to the value of the g1 variable. Once the loop cycles through all the components, all of those with a group of g2 will now have a group number specified by g1.

Listing 5.4 The RequestPermissionSlip, ReleasePermissionSlip and HavePermissionSlip functions in the GameController script.

```
function RequestPermissionSlip ( requester : GameObject )
 : boolean
{
    if ( permissionSlip == false )
    {
        permissionSlip = true;
        permissionHolder = requester;
        return true;
    } else {
        return false;
    }
}

function ReleasePermissionSlip ( requester : GameObject )
 : boolean
{
    if ( requester.GetInstanceID() ==
        permissionHolder.GetInstanceID() )
    {
        permissionSlip = false;
        permissionHolder = null;
        return true;
    } else {
        return false;
    }
```

```
}

function HavePermissionSlip ( requester : GameObject )
 : boolean
{
    if ( permissionHolder == null )
    {
        return false;
    } else {
        if ( requester.GetInstanceID() ==
            permissionHolder.GetInstanceID() )
        {
            return true;
        } else {
            return false;
        }
    }
}
```

The next task that the GameController script will manage is tracking which component has the permission to bond at any given time. This is accomplished with the three functions above. A component can receive a 'permission slip' from the game controller that gives it exclusive rights to try to bond. When one component has the permission slip, none of the others will be able to search for bonding pairs. Notice that for each of these functions, you will need to add : `boolean` after the parentheses to indicate that they will be returning either true or false.

RequestPermissionSlip is the function components will call when they want to start searching for others with which to bond. It contains an if statement that tests whether `permissionSlip` == `false`. The permissionSlip variable is a boolean that allows the game controller to remember if it has already handed out permission or not. If it hasn't it sets `permissionSlip` to `true`. Then it sets `permissionHolder` to refer to `requester` which is an argument passed into the function that refers to the component asking for permission. Then the function returns the value `true` to indicate that the requesting component now has permission to bond. If the permission slip is out, the `else` block returns `false` so the component knows not to proceed with bonding.

The ReleasePermissionSlip allows components to hand back the permission slip to the game controller. If `permissionHolder` == `null` the function returns false, since the permission slip wasn't out in the first place. Otherwise an if statement checks to see if `requester.GetInstanceID()` is the same as `permissionHolder.GetInstanceID()`. The GetInstanceID function returns a unique identification number for each game object in a scene. Comparing these two numbers confirms whether or not the component requesting to release the permission slip is the same one that currently has it. This prevents other components from accidentally releasing permission when another has it. If the two instance IDs match, the function sets `permissionSlip` to `false` and returns true, otherwise it returns false.

HavePermissionSlip offers components a way to check whether they currently have permission to execute the bonding procedure. You can see that it is nearly identical to the ReleasePermissionSlip function. The only difference is this function doesn't change the value of the permissionSlip variable. With the functions above, the game controller now has the ability to manage the component bonding process.

5.8 · Finding a Pair

Open the ComponentController script. This will be where you write the code that will give the components their intelligence. They will need to know which components they are allowed to bond with, how to choose the best one and the mechanism by which they will finally create the bond. This all starts, appropriately enough, with the Start function.

Listing 5.5 The Start function in the ComponentController script.

```
function Start ()
{
    gameController = GameObject.Find( "MainCamera" )
    .GetComponent( GameController );

    lineMaker = GameObject.Find( "LineMaker" )
    .GetComponent( LineRenderer );

    draggerController = GameObject.Find( "Dragger" )
    .GetComponent( DraggerController );

    state = ComponentState.Free;
    selectedBondingPoint = bondingPoints[0];
    bondingTimer = 0.0;
    dragging = false;
}
```

When there is a Start function in a script, its code gets executed immediately after the object it's attached to is created. This makes it a good place to set up any initial conditions that are necessary for the rest of the code to do its job. The first three statements in the code set the values of three variables – gameController, lineMaker and draggerController using the GameObject. Find function. This Find function retrieves objects in the scene by name. In this case the MainCamera, LineMaker and Dragger objects. These objects have already been created and will play various roles, as you'll see further along.

The variable state on the next line controls what actions the component can take at any given time. Setting this variable equal to ComponentState. Free means that when it's created the component will be free to start searching for other components with which to bond. There are other values for *state* that will allow objects in the scene to know whether this component is searching for a bonding pair or currently trying to bond. Using this variable will allow for coordinated action among all of the components.

The selectedBondingPoint variable will refer to one of the bonding points that you defined previously. Here it is set to bondingPoints[0], or the first bonding point in the list. As this component attempts to bond, it will try to connect to others at this location. Each time an attempt is made to bond, the component will select from its list of points one that isn't attached to another component. You'll see how this selection happens in the following sections.

Finally two variables, bondingTimer and dragging, are set to 0.0 and false respectively. The former will be used to track how long the component has been trying to bond. The later will be used to determine if the player is moving the component around using the mouse.

Listing 5.6 The Update function in the ComponentController script.

```
function Update ()
{
    if ( !gameController.paused && !gameController.frozen )
    {
        if ( state == ComponentState.Free )
        {
            if ( HasFreeBondingPoint() &&
                Random.value > 0.5 )
            {
                if ( gameController
                    .RequestPermissionSlip( gameObject ) )
```

```
                {
                    state = ComponentState.Searching;
                    StartCoroutine(
                    "FindClosestBondingPair", null );
                }
            }
        } else if ( state == ComponentState.Bonding ) {
            bondingVector = ( transform.position -
            bondingPair.transform.position ).normalized;

            bondingPair.rigidbody.velocity =
            bondingVector * bondingVelocity;

            DrawBondingLine();
        }
    }
}
```

Recall that the Update function gets called during every frame. This makes it an ideal place to continually monitor and change the state of an object. In the ComponentController script Update determines if a component should be looking for another to bond with. It also moves the component closer to its pair if it's currently trying to make a bond.

The first if statement in the function checks to make sure that the game isn't paused and that the components aren't frozen. You will be defining how gameController.paused and gameController.frozen are set a bit later on. For now, it's only important to understand that these variables should be false if the component should be allowed to do anything.

The statement if (state == ComponentState.Free) is paired with an else if statement that checks for whether state == ComponentState. Bonding is true. Since the state variable determines which actions a component is able to undertake, this if statement contains two sets of actions. If the component is free, meaning it is not searching for another component to bond with, it can start looking for a pair. If its state is bonding, then it will move closer to its chosen bonding pair.

Locate the line if (HasFreeBondingPoint() && Random.value > 0.5). This statement is located inside the block of code that will execute if the component's state is free. The HasFreeBondingPoint function will find out if this component has an available bonding point or whether it has used them all up. Random.value > 0.5 means that the code inside this if statement will

133

only execute half of the time. This randomization will ensure that the same component doesn't get chosen to bond over and over again.

If the component has a free bonding point and the random value is above 0.5, then the code proceeds to an if statement containing `gameController.RequestPermissionSlip( gameObject )`. RequestPermissionSlip is a function you will write in the GameController script. By calling this function and passing along gameObject, you are having this component ask the game controller whether it can have a turn at trying to bond. Later in this chapter you'll see how this function prevents all of the components from attempting to bond at the same time.

When the component gets permission from the game controller, it gets put into search mode with `state = ComponentState.Searching`. When a component is searching it can look for another component to bond with and others can't attempt to bond with it. After the state is set, `StartCoroutine( "FindClosestBondingPair", null )` starts the component searching for its pair. Here the StartCoroutine function calls another function named FindClosestBondingPair, which you will see below. The StartCoroutine function is used whenever an action will take a long time. In the world of software 'a long time' could be as brief as a half second. Since searching for a component to bond with could take a few seconds, StartCoroutine starts this process, but allows the Update cycle to continue. This way the action of the game will continue while this component searches for a pair.

Look inside the else if portion of the code. Here, if the state equals `ComponentState.Bonding`, the component has chosen a pair and will now try to move closer to it. To accomplish this, a variable named *bondingVector* is set equal to `(transform.position - bondingPair.transform.position).normalized`. This vector will point from the current component to bondingPair, the other component that it has chosen. It gets created by subtracting the position of the bonding pair from the position of this component. When you subtract one vector from another, the result is a new vector that points from the second to the first. The `.normalized` portion on the end of this line makes the x, y and z parameters of bondingVector all less than one. Normalizing the vector will make it easier to adjust on the next line.

After creating bondingVector, the line `bondingPair.rigidBody.velocity = bondingVector * bondingVelocity` pulls the bonding pair closer to this component. Here you are setting the velocity, or speed, of the rigid body attached to the bonding pair. The velocity of a rigid body is defined by a vector pointing in the direction of travel with a length that determines

C www. For a review of how vector mathematics works, look at Additional Resources in the Chapter 3 section of the companion website.

the rate of movement. This is calculated by multiplying bondingVector by bondingVelocity, a float. The result is the normalized vector scaled up by the value of bondingVelocity. This will determine how fast components move toward each other.

Lastly, the DrawBondingLine function is called. It will draw a line between any two components that are currently trying to bond.

Listing 5.7 The FindClosestBondingPair function in the ComponentController script.

```
function FindClosestBondingPair ()
{
    var closest_component : GameObject;
    var previous_component : GameObject;
    var closest_distance : float = Mathf.Infinity;
    var current_distance : float = 0.0;
    selectedBondingPoint = SelectBondingPoint();
    if ( selectedBondingPoint != null )
    {
        for ( var component : GameObject in
        GameObject.FindGameObjectsWithTag( "Component" ) )
        {
            if ( component
                .GetComponent( ComponentController )
                .IsAvailableToBond( gameObject,
                selectedBondingPoint.bondSet ) )
            {
                current_distance =
                (component.transform.position -
                transform.position).magnitude;

                if ( current_distance < closest_distance )
                {
                    closest_distance = current_distance;
                    if ( closest_component != null )
                    {
                        previous_component =
                        closest_component;

                        previous_component
                        .GetComponent(ComponentController)
                        .SetState( ComponentState.Free );
                    }
```

```
                closest_component = component;

                closest_component
                .GetComponent( ComponentController )
                .SetState( ComponentState.Claimed );
            }
        }
    }
    if ( closest_component == null )
    {
        state = ComponentState.Free;
    } else {
        state = ComponentState.Bonding;
        bondingPair = closest_component;

        bondingPair.GetComponent( ComponentController )
        .SetState( ComponentState.Claimed );

        bondingPair.GetComponent( ComponentController )
        .SelectBondingPoint(
        selectedBondingPoint.bondSet );

        StartBonding();
    }
} else {
    state = ComponentState.Free;
}
}
```

The code that allows a component to find a pair to bond with is contained within the FindClosestBondingPair function. There is a lot of code in this function, but its behavior is relatively simple. Each time the function is called, one of the component's bonding points is chosen in the line `selectedBondingPoint = SelectBondingPoint()`. The SelectBondingPoint function is already written for you. If you take a look at its code, you will see that it cycles through the list of bonding points and selects one that is free.

Once a bonding point is selected, the function cycles through all of the components in the beaker using a for loop. The loop defines a variable component which will represent a different component in each step of the cycle. The list of components to cycle through is created with the code `GameObject.FindGameObjectsWithTag( "Component" )`. Recall from previous chapters that this function looks for objects in the scene with the specified tag. Since all of the component objects have the "Component" tag, the result is a list that contains only the components.

For each component in the list, the first if statement inside the loop tests whether it is available to bond. The `IsAvailableToBond` function, which you'll write in the next section, asks a component whether it is currently free to bond with another component. It takes two pieces of data as arguments. The first is the component to test which is gameObject or the component to which this script is attached. The second argument is an integer that specifies a bond set. Earlier you specified this bond set number for each of the bonding points on the RoundedBar component. Two on one side of the bar were set to 1 and the two on the other side were set to 2. The bond set variable determines how two of the same type of component can bond together. If the selected bonding points of the two components are different, they can bond, otherwise they can't. Using this variable you can fine-tune the way components join together.

If the component under scrutiny is available to bond, the FindClosestBondingPair function then calculates the distance between it and the component doing the calculating. This current_distance variable will be used to determine whether this component is closer than the others in the list. The value is calculated by the code (`component.transform.position - transform.position`).`magnitude`. Subtracting the position of one from the other gives a vector between them. The magnitude gives the length of that vector, or the distance from one to the other.

Next comes the statement if (`current_distance < closest_distance`). Before the for loop, the value of closest distance is set to infinity using `Mathf.infinity`. This means that the first component the for loop looks at will be the closest, since it is less than an infinity away. As the loop progresses, each component that is closer than any of the previous options will become the new closest component.

Inside the if statement, `closest_distance` is set equal to `current_distance`, the distance to the component being evaluated. Next if the current_component variable refers to an actual component (`current_component != null`), `previous_component` is set to `current_component`. Then the state of `previous_component` is set to free using `SetState(ComponentState.Free)`, releasing it from any obligation to bond. Following this innermost if statement, `current_component` is set to `component` and its state is set via `SetState(ComponentState.Claimed)`. The claimed state ensures that this

Loops in Loops
During each frame, every component in the beaker will have a turn at executing this code. The component whose turn it is will then cycle through all the others. This loop-in-a-loop situation can be confusing. Keep in mind that the 'component under scrutiny' here is not the component currently executing this code, but one of the others.

closest component won't perform any actions while it's the best candidate for bonding.

After the for loop that cycles through the components, an if statement checks if `closest_component == null`. If this is true, it means that closest_component doesn't have a value and the code didn't find a suitable bonding pair. In this case it sets the state of this component back to free. If closest_component isn't null, the code after the `else` is triggered. The `state` of this component is set to `ComponentState.Bonding` to indicate that it is attempting to link up with another component. The `bondingPair` variable will now refer to `closest_component` object. The next line sets the `state` of `bondingPair` to `ComponentState.Claimed` indicating that it is in the process of bonding. The line after tells the bonding pair to select a compatible bonding point using `SelectBondingPoint( selectedBondingPoint.bondSet )`. This will ensure that the two components will bond using the correct bonding points. The StartBonding function that is called next initiates the bonding procedure.

The `else` block at the end of the FindClosestBondingPair function simply sets the state of this component back to free if it didn't have any bonding points available.

5.9 · Free or Otherwise

In order for a component to ascertain whether it can try to bond, it needs to know several things. It needs to know if it has a free bonding point, whether it's already bonded, what its group is and other data. The following series of functions in the ComponentController script supply this knowledge. IsAvailableToBond is the core function in this set. It will call several other functions to determine if a given component is actually ready to start the bonding procedure or not. Notice that all of the functions in this section need the `: boolean` type added after the initial parentheses.

Listing 5.8 The IsAvailableToBond function in the ComponentController script.

```
function IsAvailbleToBond (
component : GameObject, bond_set : int ) : boolean
{
    if ( state == ComponentState.Free &&
        !IsSelf( component ) &&
        !HaveAlreadyBonded( component ) &&
        !IsMemberOfGroup( component ) )
```

```
    {
        if ( component.name == gameObject.name )
        {
            if ( HasFreeBondingPoint( bond_set ) )
            {
                return true;
            } else {
                return false;
            }
        } else {
            if ( HasFreeBondingPoint() )
            {
                return true;
            } else {
                return false;
            }
        }
    } else {
        return false;
    }
}
```

IsAvailableToBond starts out with an if statement that has four conditions. Linked together with a double ampersand (&&), all of these conditions must be true in order for further tests to be performed. First the component must be free to bond. This is verified with state == ComponentState.Free. Next, the component cannot bond with itself. The condition !IsSelf(component) determines this by passing component, a variable specifying the potential bonding pair, to the function IsSelf. Third, the component cannot have already bonded with its potential pair. The condition !HaveAlreadyBonded(component) handles this. Lastly, the component cannot bond with another member of its group. This is determined by !IsMemberOfGroup(component).

If all of the above conditions are met, then a test is run to determine if component.name equals gameObject.name. These two names will be the same if the two objects were created from the same prefab. So far you are only using one component prefab, RoundedBar, so initially this will always be the case. When a component and its bonding pair are the same component type, you will need to take into account the bondingSet variable of the bonding points. The next if statement checks this with the condition HasFreeBondingPoint (bond_set). This check is here to prevent components from bonding in incorrect ways. The HasFreeBondingPoint function is already written. Take a look at it to see how it is determining which bond point to choose. If the component has a free bonding point, the function returns true and otherwise returns false.

Nearly the same lines of code are in the `else` block that appears next. The difference here is that `HasFreeBondingPoint()` is called without passing an argument. This version of the function ignores the bondingSet variable since the two components don't share the same name. Below the final `else`, the IsAvailableToBond function returns false if the initial four conditions cannot be met.

Listing 5.9 The IsSelf function in the ComponentController script.
```
function IsSelf ( other : GameObject ) : boolean
{
    if ( other.GetInstanceID() == gameObject.GetInstanceID() )
    {
        return true;
    } else {
        return false;
    }
}
```

The IsSelf function requires a game object referred to by `other`. This is the potential bonding pair for this component. An instance ID that is the same as this component's ID means it is trying to bond with itself. When this is true the function returns true, otherwise it returns false.

Listing 5.10 The HaveAlreadyBonded function in the ComponentController script.
```
function HaveAlreadyBonded ( other : GameObject ) : boolean
{
    for ( var hj : HingeJoint in
        gameObject.GetComponents( HingeJoint ) )
    {
        if ( hj.connectedBody.gameObject.GetInstanceID()
            == other.GetInstanceID() )
        {
            return true;
        }
    }
    for ( var hj : HingeJoint in
```

```
            other.GetComponents( HingeJoint ) )
    {
        if ( hj.connectedBody.gameObject.GetInstanceID()
            == gameObject.GetInstanceID() )
        {
            return true;
        }
    }
    return false;
}
```

The HaveAlreadyBonded function tests to see if this component has already created a connection with its potential bonding pair, here referred to as other. Further along you will be writing code to add hinge joints that will connect bonded pairs together. In this function, two for loops cycle through all of the hinge joints attached to each component to check whether they are already joined.

The first loop collects a list of the joints attached to this component with gameObject.GetComponents(HingeJoint). It then tests for whether the connected body is the same as other. Retrieving the ID from the hinge joint is accomplished by hj.connectedBody.gameObject.GetInstanceID(). This is necessary because the hinge joint itself doesn't know about the instance ID, only the game object has that information.

The second loop does exactly the same as the first one except it cycles through the hinge joints attached to the potential bonding pair. If at any point in either loop the instance IDs match up the function returns true indicating this component and the other have already bonded. If this doesn't happen the return false line at the end says they haven't.

Listing 5.11 The IsMemberOfGroup function in the ComponentController script.

```
function IsMemberOfGroup( other : GameObject ) : boolean
{
    if ( group == 0 &&
        other.GetComponent( ComponentController ).group == 0 )
    {
        return false;
    } else {
        if ( group ==
            other.GetComponent( ComponentController ).group )
```

```
    {
        return true;
    } else {
        return false;
    }
}
}
```

IsMemberOfGroup takes an argument named `other` and tests whether that component and this component are in the same group. If `group == 0` and `other.GetComponent( ComponentController ).group == 0`, neither component is currently in a group, so the function returns false. In the else block below, an if statement tests whether the two components have the same group number with `group == other.GetComponent( ComponentController ).group`. The function returns true, saying the two are indeed in the same group, or false that they are not.

5.10 · Starting the Bonding Process

Listing 5.12 The StartBonding function in the ComponentController script.

```
function StartBonding ()
{
    bondingVector = ( transform.position -
    bondingPair.transform.position ).normalized;

    gameController.ShowLineMaker();
}
```

Your component is finally ready to attempt bonding with other components. This process is triggered by calling the StartBonding function. This code only performs two actions. First it sets bondingVector equal to `( transform.position - bondingPair.transform.position ).normalized`. This code, which you've seen before, sets the initial direction of travel that allows the bonding pair component to start moving toward this component. The second statement, `gameController.ShowLineMaker()`, tells the game controller to turn on the line that gets drawn between the two components while they are attempting to bond.

Be sure to save your scripts, then return to Unity and press play. The components should now try to bond to each other, but they will be unsuccessful.

The code in the next sections will allow the components to finalize their bonds to each other.

5.11 · Freeze

In order for components to form bonds, it will be necessary to stop their motion temporarily. This is due to the way physics, and specifically joints, work in Unity. If two components were linked by a hinge joint immediately when they found each other, the results would be unusual. When a joint is created, the distance between the joined objects is maintained. This means that the two objects will rotate in relation to one another, but if they were some distance apart they would remain separated by that initial distance. The components in this design game are meant to be facing each other and touching at their chosen bonding points. Achieving this precision is difficult when all of the components are moving and pulling on each other. The code below allows the game controller to freeze this motion while a joint is being created. You will use it in the following sections when you write the code to create joints.

Listing 5.13 The FreezeComponents and UnfreezeComponents functions in the GameController script.

```
function FreezeComponents ()
{
    for ( var component : GameObject in
        GameObject.FindGameObjectsWithTag( "Component" ) )
    {
        component.GetComponent( ComponentController )
        .SetState( ComponentState.Free );

        component.rigidbody.isKinematic = true;
    }
    frozen = true;
    permissionSlip = false;
    HideLineMaker();
}

function UnfreezeComponents ()
{
    for ( var component : GameObject in
        GameObject.FindGameObjectsWithTag( "Component" ) )
```

```
    {
        component.rigidbody.isKinematic = false;
    }
    frozen = false;
}
```

The FreezeComponents function uses a for loop, similar to others in this chapter, that cycles through the list of components in the scene. For each component it sets the state to true using SetState(ComponentState. Free). This cancels any bonding procedures currently under way. With `component.rigidbody.isKinematic = true`, physics is disabled. This prevents the components from moving around and bumping into each other. After the for loop a variable named `frozen` is set to `true`. This allows the game controller to remember that it has frozen the components in place. The permissionSlip variable is set to false so that another component can try bonding when the components are unfrozen. Finally, `HideLineMaker()` stops the rendering of the line that gets drawn between pairs of components trying to bond.

UnfreezeComponents starts the components moving again by cycling through the list of components and setting `component.rigidbody.isKinematic` to `false`. This allows the components to start moving again. After the loop, `frozen` is set to `false` so the game controller knows that the simulation is running. Freezing and unfreezing the components will enable the code in the coming sections to properly join components together. It will also allow the player to freeze the simulation at any time to get a better look at how the components are assembling. Try this out by playing the design game, adding some components and clicking the Freeze button. You should see the components stop moving.

5.12 · Creating the Bond

Creating the actual bond between two components requires several steps. The first step is to detect when two components attempting to bond collide. Once they collide, they need to be positioned so that their selected bonding points line up perfectly. Then a joint can be created to tie the two together. The functions in this section are each responsible for a different part of this procedure.

Listing 5.14 The OnCollisionEnter function in the ComponentController script.

```
function OnCollisionEnter ( collision : Collision )
{
    if ( state == ComponentState.Bonding )
    {
        if ( collision.gameObject.GetInstanceID() ==
            bondingPair.GetInstanceID() )
        {
            CompleteBonding();
        }
    }
}
```

OnCollisionEnter gets called whenever one object runs into another object. Since the components in the simulation will be running into one another all the time, this function first checks to see that this component is bonding. Checking that `state == ComponentState.Bonding` is true ensures that only currently bonding components will actually execute the code in this function.

If the component is bonding, the next if statement checks to make sure that the object this component collided with is its bonding pair. The code `collision.gameObject` refers to the object that this component has bumped into and `bondingPair` refers to the component chosen for bonding. By comparing the instance IDs, this if statement can tell if they are the same object, or if this component has run into some other object in the scene. If this component has collided with its bonding pair, then the `CompleteBonding` function is called, which you will write next.

Listing 5.15 The CompleteBonding function in the ComponentController script.

```
function CompleteBonding ()
{
    if ( state == ComponentState.Bonding )
    {
        gameController.HideLineMaker();
        bondingTimer = 0.0;
        CreateBond();
        bondingPair.GetComponent( ComponentController )
        .CompleteBonding();
```

```
            if ( group == 0 && bondingPair
                .GetComponent( ComponentController )
                .group == 0  )
            {
                var new_group =
                gameController.GetNewGroupNumber();
                group = new_group;
                bondingPair.GetComponent( ComponentController )
                .group = new_group;
            } else if ( bondingPair
                        .GetComponent( ComponentController )
                        .group == 0  ) {
                bondingPair.GetComponent( ComponentController )
                .group = group;
            } else if ( group == 0 ) {
                group = bondingPair
                .GetComponent( ComponentController ).group;
            } else {
                gameController.MergeGroups(
                group, bondingPair
                .GetComponent( ComponentController ).group );
            }
            gameController.ReleasePermissionSlip( gameObject );
            state = ComponentState.Free;
        } else {
            bondingTimer = 0.0;
            state = ComponentState.Free;
        }
    }
}
```

The opening if statement of the CompleteBonding function checks to make sure that this component is indeed bonding. If it is, the line that gets drawn between the bonding pair is hidden using gameController.HideLineMaker. The bondingTimer is reset to 0, since this bond will now be complete. Then the CreateBond function is called to finalize everything. The line bonding-Pair.GetComponent(ComponentController).CompleteBonding() tells the bonding pair to finish its bonding process as well.

The remainder of the code in this if statement manages the process of assigning group numbers. This if statement has four blocks, each resulting in a different outcome. In the first case, both components have a group number of 0, so a new group number is assigned by the game controller. In the second case, only the bonding pair has a group number of 0, so it adopts the number of this component. In the third case only this component has a group equal to 0, so it gets assigned the bonding pair's number. The final else block takes care of the case in which both components have groups. Here the MergeGroups function in the GameController script is called to join this component's group with that of the bonding pair's.

Following the group management code, this component calls the game controller's ReleasePermissionSlip function to hand back permission to bond. Then the state is set back to free, so this component can continue to attempt bonding with others.

Listing 5.16 The CreateBond function in the ComponentController script.

```
function CreateBond ()
{
    gameController.FreezeComponents();
    PositionForBonding();
    CreateJoint();
    selectedBondingPoint.free = false;
    gameController.UnfreezeComponents();
}
```

The CreateBond function is called early in the CompleteBonding function above. It completes the bond between components. You can see that the function starts by calling FreezeComponents and ends by calling UnfreezeComponents. These two functions ensure that the components don't move while the bond is getting set up. In between the freeze and unfreeze, three actions get carried out. First, PositionForBonding is called. You will write this function next. It moves the two components so their boding points are aligned so the joint that will connect them operates correctly. CreateJoint then makes the joint, connecting the two components together. The line selectedBondingPoint.free = false, makes sure that this component doesn't try to use the chosen bonding point when it attempts to bond in the future. The next functions define how the bond between components is completed.

Listing 5.17 The PositionForBonding function in the ComponentController script.

```
function PositionForBonding ()
{
```

```
var temp_parent = GameObject();
temp_parent.transform.position = bondingPair
.GetComponent( ComponentController ).GetOffsetPosition();

temp_parent.transform.LookAt( bondingPair
.GetComponent( ComponentController )
.GetOffsetPosition() +
( bondingPair.transform.rotation * bondingPair
.GetComponent( ComponentController )
.selectedBondingPoint.jointAxis ) );

bondingPair.transform.parent = temp_parent.transform;

temp_parent.transform.position =
GetOffsetPosition() + ( transform.rotation *
selectedBondingPoint.jointAxis );

temp_parent.transform.LookAt( GetOffsetPosition() );
temp_parent.transform.position = GetOffsetPosition();
temp_parent.transform.DetachChildren();
Destroy( temp_parent );
}
```

PositionForBonding uses some vector math to determine the correct placement of the bonding pair and then moves it into position. This happens in several stages. Before the positioning starts, a GameObject named `temp_parent` is created. This is just a generic object, but it will be used to help position the bonding pair component.

First, the temp_parent has its position set to that of the bonding pair's selected bonding point. This location is retrieved using the GetOffsetPosition function in the ComponentController script attached to the bonding pair. This function is already written, but you can see how it works by navigating to it in the script. It returns the position of a component's selected bonding point, since this is the place where this component will need to move to.

Next, the `LookAt` function is called for the temp_parent. This function, part of all transform objects, takes a point in space as an argument and rotates so that it is pointing at that spot. Here the spot is just one unit off of the surface of the component. The point's position is calculated by taking the location of the selected bonding point (`GetOffsetPosition`) and adding to it. The value added is the vector resulting from multiplying the `rotation` of the component with the `jointAxis` of the component's `selectedBond-`

For a review of vector mathematics, refer to Additional Resources in the Chapter 3 section of the companion website.

ingPoint. When a rotation is multiplied with a vector, the result is the same vector rotated in space to match the rotation's angle. If the jointAxis were used without this multiplication, it might not be perpendicular to the surface of the component, which is the direction the temp_parent should be facing.

The line `bondingPair.transform.parent = temp_parent.transform` parents the bonding pair to the object created above. When one object is parented to another, a change in position of the parent also moves all of its children objects. This arrangement means that temp_parent can now be moved around, bringing the component with it.

Next, temp_parent is moved to a position just off of the surface of the component to which this script is attached. This position is calculated similarly to the point in the LookAt function. GetOffsetPosition retrieves the position of this component's selected bonding point. The rotation of this component, `transform.rotation`, is multiplied with `selectedBondingPoint.jointAxis` and the result is added to the bonding point's position. All of this yields a point just off the surface of this component, lined up with its bonding point.

The temp_parent object then gets rotated once more using the LookAt function. This time it rotates to face the selected bonding point of this component. Remember that since the bonding pair component is a child of temp_parent, it gets rotated as well. Now the two components are aligned with one another and only one unit apart.

The final move sets the position of temp_parent equal to the position of this component's selected bonding point. The line `temp_parent.DetachChildren()` then releases the bonding pair component from its parented state and `Destroy( temp_parent )` deletes the temp_parent object. The two components are now aligned and ready to get joined together.

Listing 5.18 The CreateJoint function in the ComponentController script.

```
function CreateJoint ()
{
    if ( selectedBondingPoint.jointType == JointType.Hinge )
    {
        selectedBondingPoint.joint =
        gameObject.AddComponent( HingeJoint );

        selectedBondingPoint.joint.anchor =
```

```
                selectedBondingPoint.jointPosition;

                selectedBondingPoint.joint.axis =
                selectedBondingPoint.jointAxis;

                selectedBondingPoint.joint.connectedBody =
                bondingPair.rigidbody;
        }
}
```

The final step in bonding two components together is to create the joint that will link them. In the CreateJoint function, an if statement tests if `selectedBondingPoint.jointType` is equal to `JointType.Hinge`. Hinge joints are the only type of joint used in this chapter, but this test would allow other types like spring or fixed joints to be used in the future. Inside the if statement `selectedBondingPoint.joint` gets set equal to a new joint created with `gameObject.AddComponent( HingeJoint )`. The remainder of the lines in this function configure that joint.

The location of the joint is set with `selectedBondingPoint.joint.anchor = selectedBondingPoint.jointPosition`. This is the anchor around which the components will rotate. Next the `axis` of the joint is set to `selectedBondingPoint.jointAxis`. The axis is like an axle on which the components will spin. Finally `connectedBody` is set to the `rigidbody` attached to the bonding pair. Now when joints are formed, bonded pairs will be fixed together, but able to rotate relative to each other at the position of this hinge joint.

5.13 · Giving Up

If you try playing the design game at this point you should start to see components bonding. You'll see a yellow line, created by the LineMaker object, form between bonding pairs. They will move towards each other and, if they are successful, form a joint at their selected bonding points.

You may notice as you add components to the beaker that the simulation gets stuck trying to bond two components together. This can happen when a mass of components prevents bonding pairs from reaching each other. To prevent this behavior, it will be necessary to write some code that allows components to 'give up' if the bonding process takes too long.

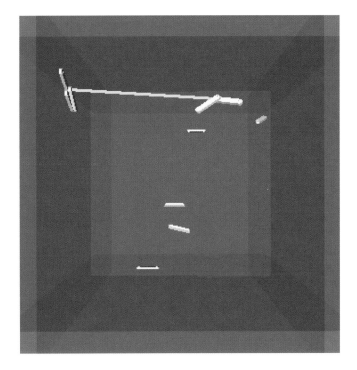

Fig. 5.5 Components bonding to each other.

Listing 5.19 Code controlling when a bonding procedure times out in the Update function of the ComponentController script.

```
function Update ()
{
    bondingTimer += Time.deltaTime;
    if ( bondingTimer >= bondingTimeLimit )
    {
        if ( state == ComponentState.Bonding )
        {
            CancelBonding();
        }
        if ( gameController.HavePermissionSlip( gameObject ) )
        {
            gameController
            .ReleasePermissionSlip( gameObject );
            state = ComponentState.Free;
        }
    }
}
```

The code above should be added at the top of the Update function in the ComponentController script. The first thing that happens is a bit of time, specified by `Time.deltaTime`, gets added to a variable named `bondingTimer`. This variable will serve as a clock to keep track of how long a component has been attempting to bond. When bondingTimer reaches a value greater than or equal (`>=`) to the value stored in `bondingTimeLimit` the code inside the first if statement executes. If the `state` of this component equals `ComponentState.Bonding`, then a function named `CancelBonding` is called. Additionally, if this component has the permission slip, it asks the game controller to release it and sets its state to free.

Listing 5.20 The CancelBonding function in the ComponentController script.

```
function CancelBonding ()
{
    if ( state == ComponentState.Bonding )
    {
        gameController.HideLineMaker();
        bondingTimer = 0.0;

        bondingPair.GetComponent( ComponentController )
        .CancelBonding();

        gameController.ReleasePermissionSlip( gameObject );
        state = ComponentState.Free;
    } else {
        bondingTimer = 0.0;
        state = ComponentState.Free;
    }
}
```

When a bonding procedure times out, the CancelBonding function resets this component's attributes so that it can try bonding with a different component. If `state == ComponentState.Bonding`, the game controller is asked to hide the line maker. The `bondingTimer` is reset to zero. The line `bondingPair.GetComponent( ComponentCOntroller ).CancelBonding()` tells the bonding pair to stop trying to bond with this component. Then the game controller is asked to release the permission slip so other components can try to bond. The code inside the else block will execute for the bonding pair, since its state is Claimed instead of Bonding. It resets the clock and sets the state to Free.

If you save the script and press play, your simulated component-molecules should now bond together much more quickly. Using the menu on the left of the screen, try adding more and more components to see what happens. You can help the simulation out by dragging components around as well. When you position the mouse cursor over a component, it will turn green indicating that you can click and drag it to a new location in the beaker.

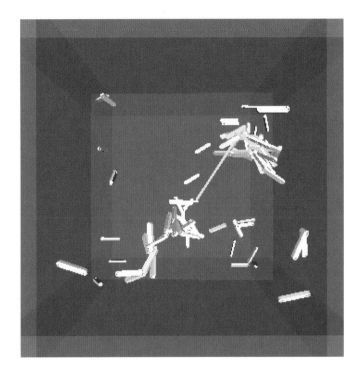

Fig. 5.6 Many components bonded together inside the beaker.

5.14 · Mix It Up

You may have noticed a few objects in the Prefabs folder that haven't been mentioned yet. There are three other components, each with different shapes, ready to be added to the design game. The names of these components are OffsetBar, VBar and QuadBar. You can see what each one looks like by selecting them in the Project View and inspecting the Preview in the Inspector.

To make these Prefabs available in the menu, you will need to add some items to the Component Prefabs and Component Icons lists. Find these lists by selecting the MainCamera in the Hierarchy and locating them in the Inspector. Change the size of each list to 4, the total number of components you will have. For the Component Prefabs list drag OffsetBar onto the 'Element 1' spot, VBar onto 'Element 2' and QuadBar onto 'Element 3'. For the Component Icons list, drag the icons corresponding to the prefabs in the same order. Your lists should look like the image in Figure 5.7.

Fig. 5.7 The Component Prefabs and Component Icons lists with four elements each.

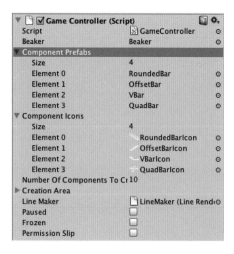

Fig. 5.8 The finished design game with different types of components bonding together.

Try it out. You should be able to add bunches of each type of component to the beaker now. See what effect adding different components in different amounts has on how assemblages are formed.

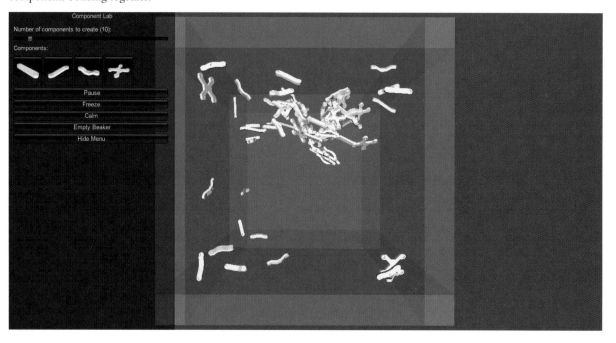

5.15 · Further Exploration

Congratulations on completing a challenging project. This design game is built with a lot of code and incorporates some tricky concepts like managing the state of objects and vector math. While you may not yet be an expert on writing code, completing this project has prepared you to take on more complex challenges as you continue to explore the possibilities that this skill opens up to you. Here are a few suggestions to keep you thinking.

- Let's say you wanted to speed up or slow down how fast the components bonded with each other. What is one variable you could change to make this happen? Hint: its name contains a synonym for speed.
- If Jessica from the brief wanted some joints to be fixed in place instead of rotating, how would you accomplish this? Where in the ComponentController script would you have to add code? Explore the Unity documentation online to find out what this type of joint is named.
- Invent a new set of components you could try out in Component Lab. What form would each one have? Where would the bonding points of each one be?

Chapter 9

SHOWROOM

6.1 · The Brief

Abbie is an architect at a firm specializing in residential design. Part of her job is to create presentations to show her clients what their new home will look like. During each client project, she typically produces several high-quality renderings showing views of the exterior of the house along with selected interior spaces. In addition to these images, she has also started producing fly-through animations that take her clients on a virtual tour through the home. Most of the positive feedback she receives from her clients is about these animations.

Even though Abbie has had success with her current techniques, she is wondering if she could improve her clients' experience even further. The fly-through visualizations offer a good overview of a design, but don't allow her clients to fully explore all of the spaces in a design. After hearing about your work with Unity, she became curious about the possibility of making her visualizations more like video games. She thinks that by offering her clients a game that encourages them to thoroughly explore their future home they will understand her design decisions more fully. This would lead to better communication between her and her clients about what aspects in a design might need to change. A quick fly-through of a kitchen might not accomplish much, but walking through and interacting with the space might reveal new opportunities to make the space function better.

6.2 · The Proposal

The first step in creating Abbie's design game will be to allow a player to explore her design like in a video game. Abbie has already provided you with a 3D model of her design. You will need to do some additional preparation to create a sense of realistic movement within the spaces. You will use some standard Unity functionality to create a first-person avatar that will enable the player to 'walk' from space to space in the house. The 3D geometry of the model will need some additional components to prevent this avatar from falling through the floor or passing through walls.

Next you will use some more advanced features to display Abbie's design in a visually appealing manner. She wants the spaces to have realistic lighting that will accentuate the layout and materials she has chosen for the design. You will be adding lights to the scene and tuning them to achieve the best effect. You will also learn about lightmapping, a technique for embedding these lighting effects directly into the model itself.

Finally you will add the incentives to explore the entire house. These incentives will take the form of a kind of scavenger hunt. Players will see goals scattered throughout the house. The goals will be associated with key design features of the house and, when reached by the player, offer further details. Once the player has reached all of the goals, they've won the game.

6.3 · Opening the Project

Open the ShowroomStarter project in Unity. Make sure that the Level1 scene is open by double-clicking on it in the Project View. Unlike in past projects, this scene is quite empty; there isn't even a camera or a light. You will be populating most of this scene from scratch. Familiarize yourself with the items in the Project View. The first item of interest is the Apartment01 model, which you will find in the Models folder.

6.4 · Adding the Model

Drag the Apartment01 model into the Hierarchy to add it to the scene. It is located inside a folder named Apartment01, alongside folders for materials and textures that the model uses.

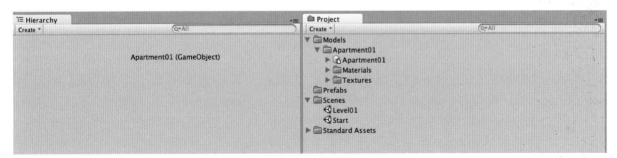

Fig. 6.1 Adding the Apartment01 model to the scene.

If your view into the scene is positioned correctly, the Scene View should be showing the interior of the model. If you are looking at the outside, use the pan, look and zoom tools from the Toolbar to get a better view. The model is of an apartment that Abbie has redesigned for some of her clients.

Because there are no light sources anywhere in the scene, your first view of the model will be rather dark. To fix this, you can add a light that will mimic the rays of a table lamp. Pan and zoom to get a better view of the small

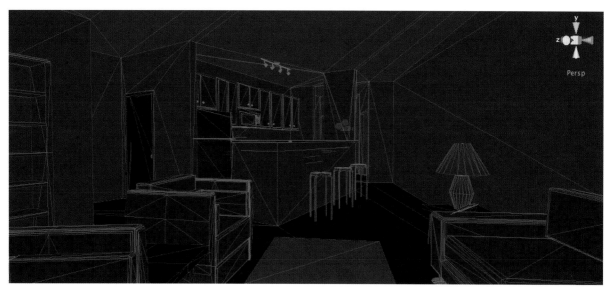

Fig. 6.2 A dark and gloomy view of the interior of the model. The blue lines indicate that the model is selected in the Hierarchy.

Fig. 6.3 Positioning a spotlight as it looks normally (left) and the small square that appears when Shift and Control are held down (right).

lamp with a conical shade on the coffee table next to the sofa. Once your view is positioned in front of the table lamp, select **Game Object > Create Other > Spotlight** from the main menu. Set the rotation of the light in the Inspector to (90, 0, 0) so its light is cast downward. The spotlight should be relatively close to the table lamp, but will probably need to be repositioned so it appears where the light bulb would be placed. Positioning objects precisely in the Scene View can be a bit difficult. With the translate button selected in the Toolbar, hold down the Shift and Control keys. Now drag the square in the center of the translate gizmo. In this mode, the object you are moving will 'snap' to nearby surfaces.

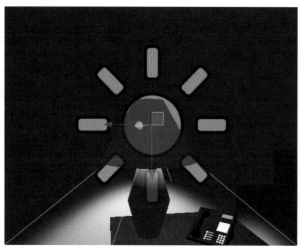
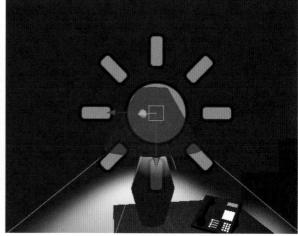

This technique requires some practice to master. Changing your view into the scene from one side of the lamp to the other will help you verify that the light is in the correct position. Once the placement seems correct using the right, green or blue arrows can help fine-tune this position. Increase the Spot Angle of the light in the Inspector to broaden its coverage. Rename this light 'TableLight' in the Hierarchy, so you can identify it later. You will add more lights to the scene using this same technique later in this chapter.

www. For extra help with positioning the light, see Additional Resources in the Chapter 6 section of the companion website.

6.5 · Moving Around

If the client-players are to be able to move around this apartment like in a video game, they will need a mechanism for doing so. You can create such a mechanism by adding two objects and some code. Start by selecting **GameObject > Create Empty** from the main menu. Rename this object 'Player' in the Hierarchy, since it will form the root object that will allow movement around the scene. In the Inspector, set its position to (−1.5, 1.6, −4.6). This will start the player out by the apartment's entrance.

Next select **GameObject > Create Other > Camera** from the main menu. This camera will serve as the player's eyes as they move around the scene. Make the Player the parent of the camera by dragging the Camera object onto the Player object in the Hierarchy. Select the Camera and set its position to (0, 0, 0). Now the camera and the player are in the same position. The player will move around the scene and the camera will tilt to offer a better view.

Find the PlayerController script in the Project View and attach it by dragging it onto the Player object in the Hierarchy. Open up the script and add the following code to the Update function.

Listing 6.1 The Update function in the PlayerController script.

```
function Update ()
{
    movement = Vector3.zero;
    if ( Input.GetKey( KeyCode.UpArrow ) )
    {
        movement = transform.forward * velocity;
    }
    if ( Input.GetKey( KeyCode.DownArrow ) )
    {
        movement = transform.forward * -velocity;
```

```
        }
        if ( Input.GetKey( KeyCode.RightArrow ) )
        {
            movement = transform.right * velocity;
        }
        if ( Input.GetKey( KeyCode.LeftArrow ) )
        {
            movement = transform.right * -velocity;
        }
        if ( movement.magnitude > 0 )
        {
            transform.position += movement;
        }
        if ( Input.GetKey( KeyCode.D ) )
        {
            transform.localRotation.y += angularVelocity;
        }
        if ( Input.GetKey( KeyCode.A ) )
        {
            transform.localRotation.y -= angularVelocity;
        }
        if ( Input.GetKey( KeyCode.W ) )
        {
            playerCamera.localRotation.x -= angularVelocity;
        }
        if ( Input.GetKey( KeyCode.S ) )
        {
            playerCamera.localRotation.x += angularVelocity;
        }
}
```

There are several lines of code here, but its purpose is simple. The action of the player will be driven by two sets of keyboard keys. The arrow keys will control forward, backward, left and right motion. The A, W, S, D keys will control the angle of view.

The first four if statements check for whether any of the up, down, right or left arrow keys are being pressed. Inside each a vector named movement is assigned a value. For instance, if the up arrow is pressed, movement is set to transform.forward * velocity. The vector transform.forward always points straight ahead of the object this script is attached to; in this case the player. Multiplying this vector by the velocity variable means that as long as the up arrow is being pressed, the player will move forward at a constant speed. Notice that when the down arrow is pressed `transform.forward` is multiplied by `-velocity`. This will cause the player to move in reverse. When the right or left arrow keys are pressed the vector `transform.right` is used. This has the effect of moving the player to the right (`velocity`) or the left (`-velocity`). The movement is ultimately applied in the line `transform.position += movement`.

The A, S, W, D keys control rotation. The D and A keys add or subtract a small amount of rotation, stored in the `angularVelocity` variable, to `transform.localRotation.y` to make the view swing to the right or left. The W and S keys do much the same, but with `playerCamera.localRotation.x`. This allows the camera to move up and down without changing the transform.forward vector of the player. If that were allowed to happen, the player would veer into the floor or the ceiling.

With the Player highlighted in the Inspector, drag the Camera object onto the line that reads 'Player Camera' in the Inspector. Additionally, set the Velocity to 0.05 and the Angular Velocity to 0.03. These settings will ensure the player's movements are not too rapid. Try playing the game to get a feel for how these controls work.

Fig. 6.4 Navigating the scene with the arrow and A, W, S, D keys.

6.6 · Let There Be Light

If this space is to have the aesthetic that Abbie is looking for, it will need a few more lights. In this section you will add lights that will simulate the effect that the fixtures in the apartment would have. There are several light fixtures in the apartment model. See if you can spot them all. Besides the table lamp you have already lit, there are seven others. Four lights are attached to a track on the ceiling in the kitchen. Three lights with cylindrical shades hang from the ceiling at the entrance, in the living room and in the bedroom.

To start, place spotlights in each light fixture attached to the track in the kitchen. Change your perspective in the Scene View until you have a close view of the track.

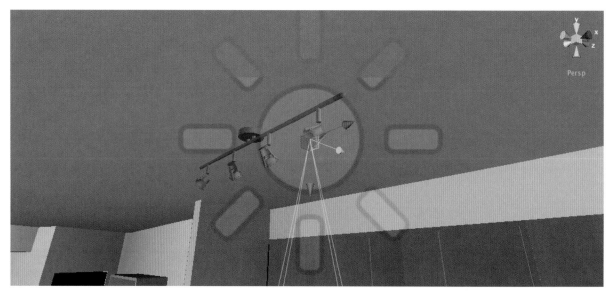

Fig. 6.5 Positioning a spotlight in the first track light fixture.

Add a spot light to the scene by choosing **GameObject > Create Other > Spotlight** from the main menu. The new spotlight should appear directly in front of you in the Scene View. Using the technique you learned earlier in this chapter, position the spotlight so it snaps to the position of the first track light. Select the Rotate tool from the Toolbar and change the orientation of the spotlight such that it aligns with the light fixture. Altering your

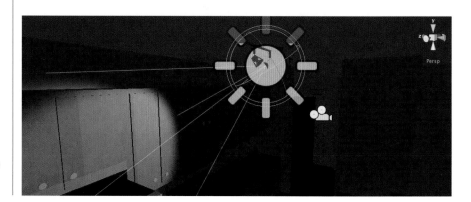

Fig. 6.6 Rotating a spotlight into position. The yellow lines indicate the cone of light that is emitted.

view of the fixture will help you achieve an accurate position and rotation for the spotlight. Set the Spot Angle of the spotlight to 60 degrees so it casts its light more widely.

Each fixture in the track light will require you to create a new spotlight, position it, rotate it and set its spot angle. By paying close attention to these details, you should be able to achieve a fairly realistic effect from the track lights.

Fig. 6.7 The kitchen lit by four track light fixtures, each with a spotlight.

6.7 · Overhead Lights

The next light you will create is for the hanging light fixture in the living room directly above the table between the sofa and two chairs. This fixture has a cylindrical shade that allows for a wider angle than the table lamp. Change your perspective in the Scene View so this fixture is in the center of your view.

Fig. 6.8 The cylindrically shaded fixture on the living room ceiling.

For this fixture, you'll create a point light that casts light in all directions. This will more accurately simulate the type of light cast from a fixture like this. Add the point light by selecting **Game Object > Create Other > Point Light** from the main menu. Use the same steps as in the previous section to position the light in the center of the cylindrical shade. Use the Scene Gizmo to cycle through the various views until you're satisfied that the point light is positioned correctly.

Since a point light casts light in all directions, it doesn't have an angle associated with it. It does, however, have an intensity. Intensity is a parameter that all lights have. It determines how bright a light shines. The default intensity for point lights is one, but this value makes the light brighter than it needs to be. With the point light highlighted in the Hierarchy, change its intensity to 0.5. This will give off the subtle, ambient light intended by the designer.

Learn more about lights in Unity by looking at Additional Resources in the Chapter 6 section of the companion website.

Fig. 6.9 The living room now lit by the overhead cylindrical light fixture.

Locate the other two light fixtures like this one. One is located on the bedroom ceiling. The other is on the ceiling by the entrance door. Create two point lights with the same attributes as the one you just made. Position them in the centers of those light fixtures.

Fig. 6.10 The light fixture in the bedroom (left) and another near the entrance (right).

6.8 · The First Goal

To encourage players to fully explore the apartment, you will add some goals at various points throughout the space. Each goal will inform the player about an aspect of the design and spur them on to learn more. Goals will take the form of animated arrows pointing out the areas of interest in the apartment. When the player finds and clicks on all of the goals, they will be rewarded with a surprise.

Create an empty object by selecting **GameObject > Create Empty**. Position this object at the origin (0, 0, 0) and rename it 'Goal'. In the Project View, locate the Arrow prefab inside the Models folder. Create a copy by dragging it into the Hierarchy. With the Arrow still highlighted in the Hierarchy, drag it onto the Goal object and set its position to (0, 0, 0). Change your perspective in the Scene View so you're looking at the arrow. It will be just outside the entrance to the apartment. The player will eventually need to click on the arrow and this requires a collider. Add one by highlighting Goal in the Hierarchy and selecting **Component > Physics > Box Collider**. In the Inspector set the box collider's Size to (0.6, 2, 0.2). This will provide a large target for the players to click.

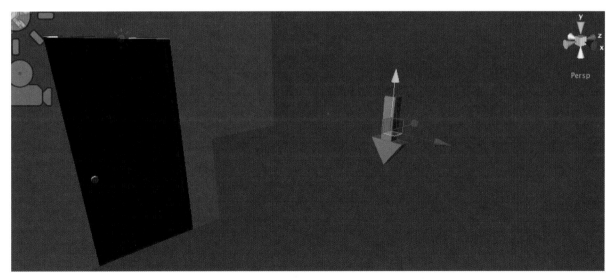

Fig. 6.11 The arrow outside the entrance to the apartment.

To make the goal attractive to players, you will employ Unity's animation capabilities. With the Arrow highlighted in the Hierarchy, select **Window > Animation** from the main menu. You will animate the arrow here at the origin, make a prefab and then create several copies.

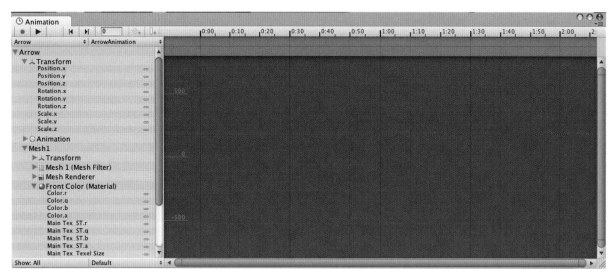

Fig. 6.12 The Animation window.

Using this window, you can create animations that make objects move, change color, grow, spin and more. It can be tricky to understand at first, but it is a powerful tool that can accomplish many complex actions without the need for writing code. Along the top of the animation window is a timeline, graduated in seconds that determines how long an action takes. Along the left side are the different parameters that can be animated. For the arrow, you'll create an animation that causes it to bounce and change color over time.

In the Animation Window, locate the blank menu to the right of the menu that reads 'Arrow'. Click this menu and select 'Create New Clip'. When you are asked to save your new clip, name it 'GoalAnimation'.

For an overview of the animation window, see Additional Resources in the Chapter 6 section of the companion website.

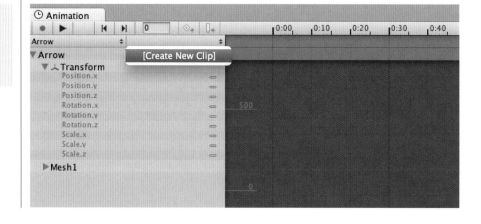

Fig. 6.13 Creating a new animation clip.

On the left side of the animation window, locate the line that reads 'Position.y'. Right-click on this line and select 'Add Curves'. This will populate the timeline portion of the window with lines corresponding to the x, y and z position of the arrow over time. A diamond icon will also be placed at the beginning of the timeline. Diamond icons indicate a keyframe or a point in time when a parameter can be fixed at a specific value.

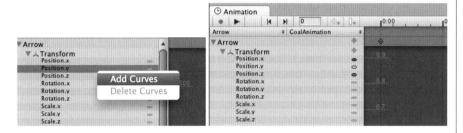

Fig. 6.14 Adding curves (left) and the diamond icon that appears as a result (right).

Since the arrow should also change color, you will need to add curves for those values as well. Click the triangle icon on the 'Mesh 1' line, then the triangle icon on the 'Front Color' line to show the lines that control color for the arrow. By highlighting the four color lines (shift-click), then right-clicking and selecting 'Add Curves', the colors will be added to the timeline along with the position.

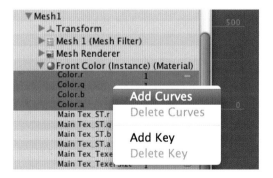

Fig. 6.15 Adding curves for the color parameters.

Any animation requires both a starting time and an ending time. Both of these points will be keyframes, defining how long the animation lasts. The beginning of this animation has been created at time 0:00 simply by selecting 'Add Curves'. To define the end, you will need to position the play head (represented by the red line) at the end time and add a keyframe. Do this by clicking on the red line in the light gray bar containing the numbers (0:00, 0:10, 0:20, etc.) and dragging it to the right until it lines up with one second (1:00).

Fig. 6.16 Dragging the play head from 0:00 to 1:00.

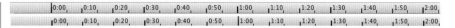

Make sure that none of the parameters on the right are selected by clicking on a blank spot in the right panel of the animation window.

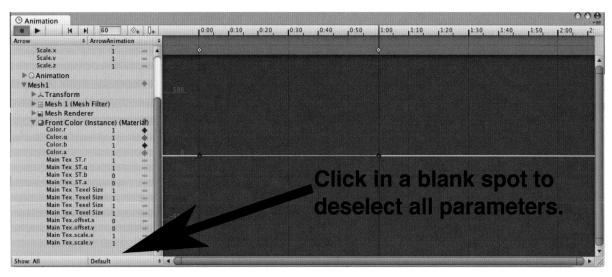

Fig. 6.17 Deselecting parameters in the animation window.

Once the play head is at one second, you can add a keyframe by clicking the diamond icon to the right of the timeline ( ). Now the animation has a beginning and an end. Click on the diamond icon just below the 1:00 in the timeline to select that keyframe. Now, in the right panel, change the value of Position.y to 1. By setting this value the animation will move the arrow from a starting position of 0.8 to a position one second later of 1.0. If you click the play button at the top right of the animation window and look at the Scene View, you should see the arrow rise.

Fig. 6.18 Deselected (left) and selected (right) keyframes.

To make the arrow bounce, it's necessary to repeat this action, except in reverse. You can achieve this by selecting 'Ping Pong' from the menu in the lower left that reads 'Default'. The options in this menu define how an animation behaves. By default, animations will play only once. With the play mode set to 'Ping Pong', this animation will play through the defined animation, play it in reverse and then repeat this cycle forever. Save the animation

(Ctrl-S or Cmd-S) and return to the Unity window. Press play and look at the arrow over the table to see the animation in action.

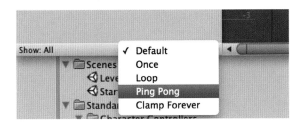

Fig. 6.19 Selecting Ping Pong from the animation playback mode menu.

Animating color requires the same basic steps as animating position. Return to the animation window and select the keyframe at one second. Click the record button ( ) to ensure that you can edit the animation. In the right panel of the animation window, change the value of Color.b to 0. Save the animation and press play in the Animation Window to see the arrow bounce and turn from white to yellow.

The animation system in Unity can change the values for nearly every parameter associated with an object. Scale, rotation, light intensity, textures and more can be animated over time to achieve a variety of effects.

6.9 · Reaching the Goal

Now that you've created a goal, you need to give the player a way to record that they've reached it. Take a look in the Project View and find the GoalController script inside the Scripts folder. Attach this script to the Goal object in the Hierarchy.

Listing 6.2 The OnMouseUp and OnGUI functions in the GoalController script.

```
function OnMouseUp ()
{
    if ( !displayMessage )
    {
        displayMessage = true;
    }
}

function OnGUI ()
{
    if ( displayMessage )
```

```
        {
            GUI.Box( Rect( Screen.width * 0.5 - 200,
                           Screen.height * 0.5 - 200,
                           400, 400 ),
                     "You've reached a goal!" );
            GUI.Label( Rect( Screen.width * 0.5 - 170,
                             Screen.height * 0.5 - 170,
                             340, 340 ),
                       message );
        }
    }
}
```

Add the code above to the GoalController script. The OnMouseUp function will get called whenever the player clicks on the Arrow. Inside, an if statement checks the value of a variable named displayMessage. If the value of this variable is false, it is changed to true.

The OnGUI function makes use of the displayMessage variable by showing a message on the screen when it's true. It draws two elements on the screen, a box and a label, using GUI.Box and GUI.Label respectively. Both of these functions require two arguments. One is a rectangle that defines their placement and size, and the other is some text. The Rect that is created for the box places it in the middle of the screen and gives it a size of 400 by 400 pixels. The label is positioned and sized so that it fits within the boundaries of the box. The text for the box, "You've reached a goal!", will appear at the top as a title.

To finalize the Goal, create a prefab in the Project View and name it 'Goal'. Drag the Goal object from the Hierarchy to the newly created prefab. Now you will be able to create new copies of the goal around the apartment. Position your view so you can see the kitchen clearly. Drag the Goal prefab

Fig. 6.20 A copy of the Goal prefab positioned in the middle of the kitchen floor.

from the Project View directly into the Scene View. This is a quick way to create new objects and position them at the same time.

Some text will appear whenever a player clicks on a goal. This is determined by the value of a variable named `message` in the GoalController script. With the new Goal highlighted in the Hierarchy, locate the Message line in the Inspector. Type in some descriptive text about the kitchen. Check to see that the message is working by pressing play, navigating so you can see the arrow, then clicking it. You should see the message you entered appear in the middle of the screen.

Fig. 6.21 The message displayed when a player clicks the goal.

There is one small problem. Once the message is displayed, it stays on the screen forever. Fixing this is a simple task that requires just a bit of code.

Listing 6.3 The Update function in the GoalController script.

```
function Update ()
{
    if ( displayMessage )
    {
        timer += Time.deltaTime;
        if ( timer > 5.0 )
```

```
                {
                    displayMessage = false;
                    Destroy( gameObject );
                }
            }
        }
```

This code in the Update function tracks how long the message has been displayed and turns it off after five seconds. If `displayMessage` is true, `Time.deltaTime` is added to `timer`. This variable stores the amount of time in seconds since the message was displayed. Once it is greater than `5.0`, `displayMessage` is set to `false`. Since this goal has been reached, the arrow gets deleted by `Destroy( gameObject )`. If you press play again, you should see the message and the arrow disappear after five seconds.

6.10 · Adding More Goals

A game with only a single goal isn't much fun. In this section you will add two more to encourage players to fully explore the apartment. Position your view just in front of the table in the living room between the sofa and chairs. Drag a copy of the Goal prefab from the Project View into the Scene View. Position the arrow that gets created just above the table. Change the y-axis rotation of this goal so the flat side faces toward your view point.

Fig. 6.22 The second goal positioned above the living room table.

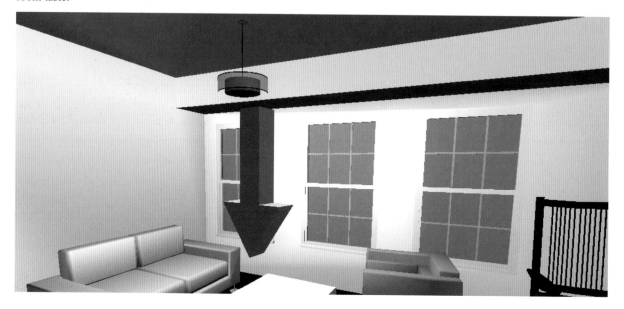

Give this goal a message describing the living room furniture. With the new Goal object highlighted in the Hierarchy, change the text on the Message line in the Inspector. Verify that this new goal is behaving as expected by pressing play and clicking on it.

The third and final goal will go in the bedroom. Position your view and drag the Goal prefab into the Scene View once again to position the new arrow above the bed. The goal can have a message about the furniture, lighting or other aspects of the room. The goal of the message is to convey information to the player that they wouldn't otherwise know. Test this goal out to make sure it's working.

Fig. 6.23 The goal in the bedroom.

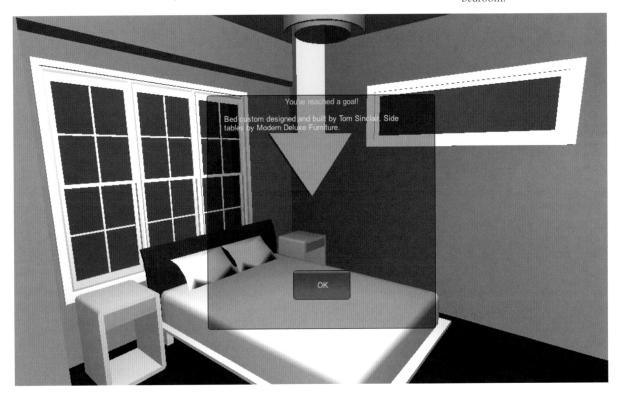

6.11 · Completing the Level

To provide the player with a sense of accomplishment, you can add a finale to this level. Adding an ending requires that your game keep track of the player's progress. All three goals need to be reached in order for the player to win. You will need a mechanism to count how far along the player is and trigger the finale once the level is complete. Open the GameController script and add the following code.

Listing 6.4 The ReachedGoal and OnGUI functions of the GameController script.

```
function ReachedGoal ()
{
    goalsReached++;
    if ( goalsReached == totalGoals )
    {
        displayEnding = true;
        endingGraphics.SetActiveRecursively( true );
    }
}

function OnGUI ()
{
    if ( displayEnding )
    {
        GUI.Box( Rect( Screen.width * 0.5 - 200,
                       Screen.height * 0.5 - 100,
                       400, 200 ),
                 "You've reached all the goals!" );
    }
}
```

The GameController script is attached to an empty object by the same name that is already in the scene. This object is invisible, but will keep track of the player's progress through this level.

The ReachedGoal function will be called whenever the player clicks on a goal. It increments an integer variable named goalsReached by 1 (++). Then an if statement tests whether goalsReached is equal to totalGoals. The total goals is equal to three currently. If you were to add more goals, you would change this value in the Inspector. If the player has clicked on every goal, the function then sets displayEnding to true. It also calls the function SetActiveRecursively(true) on a game object referred to by endingGraphics. SetActiveRecursively turns objects off when it's passed a false value and on when passed true. Since this object will be hidden until the level is complete, true is used. You will create the endingGraphics object a bit later.

The OnGUI function waits until the value of displayEnding is true. Once it is, a box is created in the middle of the screen with the message "You've reached all the goals!". Test this behavior out by playing the

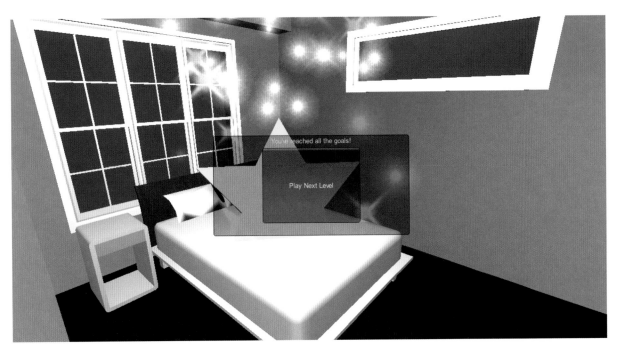

Fig. 6.24 The ending displayed once all the goals have been reached.

design game and clicking each of the arrows in the scene. You should see the message appear on the screen.

6.12 · Further Exploration

Congratulations on successfully completing yet another project. In this chapter you have learned about lighting, animation and particles. If you continue to develop your skills using Unity, you will discover the amazing variety of effects you can achieve with these techniques.

- Let's say Abbie from the Brief wanted the player to be able to change the intensity or orientation of the lights in the apartment. How could you accomplish this? What kind of interface would you offer the player that would allow them to change these attributes?
- Think of a way you could simulate daytime and nighttime in this design game. How would you change the lighting to best emulate these two conditions?
- If you added a model of a chair to the scene, what components would you need to attach to it that would allow the player to bump into and move it?

Conclusion

My goal in writing this book hasn't been to turn you into a professional game developer. Rather, I'm interested in teaching designers how to harness the powerful tools that are so prevalent in game development so they can invent new ways of designing. The host of software that designers have at their disposal offers a wide array of capabilities. Software to model 3D forms, create precise 2D drawings, modify images and edit video are extremely powerful today. Most of this software, however, is optimized for accelerating the pace of production. The projects in this book, on the other hand, were conceived to open up new creative avenues. Folding paper and simulating molecular bonding may seem like strange methods for arriving at design solutions, but whenever concepts like these are imported into the design process, unintentional shifts in thinking are bound to happen.

Making tools for drawing, form creation and communication behave more like video games isn't just about making them more fun to use, though this is one of the great benefits. It's also about making them more unpredictable, more surprising. Most designers will tell you that serendipity plays a big role in their design process. Meeting people from different professions, reading books on disparate subjects and embracing new ways of creating can dramatically impact the type of work a designer produces. We will always need straightforward, powerful and efficient tools to move our designs from conception to completion. But what if more of our tools embraced a bit of randomness, self-organization and serendipity?

Video games are designed with this sort of controlled unpredictability. It's not that anything is possible, but that within the constraints of the game there is a wide enough range of possibilities such that no two sessions ever turn out quite the same. This is the type of variation that can drive creativity in design processes, particularly at the concept stage. By building tools that are played rather than simply used, we could expand the boundaries of our creativity by allowing our tools to influence us as much as we control them. If just one great design idea emerged out of this play, it would make all of the effort worth it.

Where are the opportunities for play in your design process? Whether you design lighting fixtures or skyscrapers, there are hundreds of opportunities to inject some serendipity. Think about the way an architect's desk lamp is assembled. Could you envision a way to use the ideas from the Component Lab project to play around with how the pieces of the lamp get assembled? Suppose you're designing the facade of a building. What implications might Kirigami have on the process of creating that surface? There are opportunities in communication as well. What if you used the methods in Showroom to let your clients or your boss experience a new design?

The important idea here is not to build design games that create a finished product for you. Instead it's about finding specific opportunities to expand the choices you have in your design decisions. The products that come out of design games aren't an end, they're a beginning. Design games are about producing the seeds of inspiration for a design. The more seeds you can produce, the more options you'll have in choosing a place to start your project. These initial ideas can then form the basis for further exploration. Just maybe one of them might change your entire way of thinking about a design challenge.

As you move ahead, keep the skills and ideas you've acquired from this book in mind. When you play video games, take note of what makes them fun, motivating and captivating. One of these ideas or techniques may form the basis for your next design game. In the meantime keep playing, inventing and having fun.

Further Reading

More About Game Design

These books offer a variety of viewpoints on what makes games fun and compelling. Some approach the subject from a technical standpoint, while others explore psychological and social aspects. They also offer specific, time-tested techniques for designing games that are engaging.

Bogost, Ian. *How to Do Things with Video Games*. Minneapolis: University of Minnesota Press, 2011.

Fullerton, Tracy. *Game Design Workshop: A Playcentric Approach to Creating Innovative Games*. New York: CRC Press, 2008.

McGonigal, Jane. *Reality is Broken: How Games Make Us Better and How They Can Change the World*. New York: Penguin Books, 2011.

Salen, Katie and Zimmerman, Eric. *Rules of Play: Game Design Fundamentals*. Cambridge, MA: MIT Press, 2003.

Schell, Jesse. *The Art of Game Design: A Book of Lenses*. Burlington, MA: Morgan Kaufmann, 2008.

More About Unity

There is a lot more of Unity to explore. By reading these books, you will discover additional techniques to enrich your design games. Oriented toward video game development, they offer instruction on programming behavior, creating visual effects, incorporating sound and more.

Creighton, Ryan. *Unity 3D Game Development by Example: Beginner's Guide.* Birmingham, UK: Packt Publishing, 2010.

de Byl, Penny. *Holistic Game Development with Unity: An All-in-one Guide to Implementing Game Mechanics, Art, Design and Programming.* Waltham, MA: Focal Press, 2011.

Goldstone, Will. *Unity 3.x Game Development Essentials.* Birmingham, UK: Packt Publishing, 2011.

Other Technologies

While there are virtually infinite other technologies out there to learn, the ones presented in these books may be of particular interest to you. They present development platforms that are used by designers, artists, information visualizers and other creative coders. You will discover new programming languages and techniques to link your design games to the physical world through electronics, sensors and other devices.

Fry, Ben. *Visualizing Data: Exploring and Explaining Data with the Processing Environment.* Sebastopol, CA: O'Reilly Media, 2008.

Kean, Sean, Hall, Jonathan and Perry, Phoenix. *Meet the Kinect: An Introduction to Programming Natural User Interfaces.* New York: Apress, 2011.

Klanten, Robert, et al. *A Touch of Code: Interactive Installations and Experiences.* Berlin: Die Gestalten Verlag, 2011.

Lieberman, Zachary. *Getting Started with openFrameworks.* Sebastopol, CA: O'Reilly Media, 2013.

Noble, Joshua. *Programming Interactivity: A Designer's Guide to Processing, Arduino and Openframeworks.* Sebastopol, CA: O'Reilly Media, 2009.

Noble, Joshua and Hodgin, Robert. *Exploring Cinder.* Sebastopol, CA: O'Reilly Media 2013.

Raes, Casey and Fry, Ben. *Processing: A Programming Handbook for Visual Designers and Artists.* Cambridge, MA: MIT Press, 2011.

Shiffman, Daniel. *Nature of Code: Simulating Natural Systems with Processing.* The Nature of Code, 2012.

Terzidis, Kostas. *Algorithms for Visual Design Using the Processing Language.* Indianapolis, IN: Wiley, 2009.

Index

Note: Page numbers followed by 'f' refer to figures.